Classics In
Child Development

Classics In
Child Development

Advisory Editors

JUDITH KRIEGER GARDNER
HOWARD GARDNER

Editorial Board

Wayne Dennis
Jerome Kagan
Sheldon White

STUDIES OF

PLAY

Library
S.W. Ok. St. U.
Weatherford, Oklahoma

ARNO PRESS

A New York Times Company

New York — 1975

Reprint Edition 1975 by Arno Press Inc.

Copyright © 1975, by W. W. Norton & Company, Inc.

Reprinted by permission of W. W. Norton & Company, Inc.

Classics in Child Development
ISBN for complete set: 0-405-06450-0
See last pages of this volume for titles.

Manufactured in the United States of America

Library of Congress Cataloging in Publication Data

Erikson, Erik Homburger, 1902-
    Studies of play.

    (Classics in child development)
    Reprint of the author's Configurations in play,
originally published in Psychoanalytic quarterly, v. 6
and his Studies in the interpretation of play, originally
published in Genetic psychology monographs, v. 22, no. 4,
1939.
    1. Play. I. Erikson, Erik Homburger, 1902-
Studies in the interpretation of play. 1975. II. Title.
III. Series.
BF717.E74 1975   155.4'1   74-21429
ISBN 0-405-06478-0

155.41
Er46s

CONTENTS

207317

CONFIGURATIONS IN PLAY
—CLINICAL NOTES

CONFIGURATIONS IN PLAY —CLINICAL NOTES

BY ERIK HOMBURGER (NEW HAVEN, CONN.)

INTRODUCTION

Listening to an adult's description of his life, we find that a clear vista into his past is limited by horizons: one is the onset of puberty, with its nebulous "screen memories", another the onset of the so-called latency period through which, in retrospect, memories appear inaccurate and obscure, if at all. In our work with children we meet another horizon, the period of language development. "The material which the child furnishes us," says Anna Freud in her Introduction to the Technic of Child Analysis, "supplies us with many welcome confirmations of facts which up to the present moment we have only been able to maintain by reference to adult analysis. But . . . it does not lead us beyond the boundary where the child becomes capable of speech; in short, that time from whence on its thinking becomes analogous to ours." [1]

Associations, fantasies, dreams, lead in the analysis of the adult mind to the land beyond the mountains; in child analysis these roads lose their reliability and have to be supplemented by others, especially the sequences which occur spontaneously in the child's play.

It seems to me, however, that when substituting play for other associative material we are inclined to apply to its observation and interpretation methods which do not quite do justice to its nature. We tend to neglect the characteristic which most clearly differentiates play from the world of psychological data communicated to us by means of language, namely, the manifestation of an experience in actual space, in

---

[1] Freud, Anna: *Introduction to the Technic of Child Analysis.* **Nervous and Mental Disease** Monograph Series No. 48, 1928. p. 43.

the dynamic relationship of shapes, sizes, distances—in what we may call *spatial configurations.*

In the following notes it is hoped to draw attention to this spatial aspect of play as the element which is of dominant importance in the specificity of *"Spiel-Arbeit"*. These notes are based on observations made for the most part in the twilight of clinical experience, and must be supplemented by systematic work with normal or only slightly disturbed children. For although the adult who is not an artist must undergo the specific psychoanalytic procedure in order to reveal his unconscious in the play of ideas (a procedure which cannot easily be replaced for "scientific purposes" by less intimate and more systematic arrangements), the child in his play continuously and naturally "weaves fantasies around real objects".[1]

I.
"HOUSES"

1.

An anxious and inhibited four-year-old boy, A, comes for observation. The worried mother has told us: (1) that he is afraid to climb stairs or to cross open spaces; (2) that as a baby he had eczema and that for eight months his arms were often tied in order to prevent his scratching; and (3) that until recently he continued to wet himself, with a climax at the time of a younger sister's arrival.

Let us see what he shows in the first minutes of play. Taking a toy house he places three bears close together in one corner. The father bear is lying in the bathtub, the mother

---

[1] Wälder, Robert: *The Psychoanalytic Theory of Play.* This QUARTERLY, II.
According to the current theories of play, either the past, "a pressure exerted by unfinished processes", leads the playing child's mind to the *mastery through repetition* of traumatic experiences: "adding an *active counterpart to the passive experience*" (Freud); or the present is in the lead insisting on the *discharge of surplus energy*, on the fulfilment of wishes here and now, or on *functional pleasure* (Buehler, in Wälder's formulation: "pleasure experienced in pure performance without regard to the success of activity"); finally, it may be the future and its tasks for which the child may be training himself in the trials, errors and victories of his play experimentation (Groos).

bear is washing at the sink, while the baby bear is drinking water. The emphasis on water reminds us of the boy's urinary difficulty. It also must mean something that the family is placed so close together, for he then arranges a group of animals outside the house equally close to one another. "Can you build a cage around these animals?" he asks me. Provided with blocks, he builds the "cage" shown in Figure 1 *beside*

FIGURE 1

them—a house-form which on a normative scale of infantile house-building would belong to a much younger age. At five one knows that a house is "around something"; but A has forgotten the animals. He seems to use the blocks in order to express the *feeling of being caged;* he even places a small picture frame which he finds among the toys around the cage itself. Thus he is indicating in the *content* of his play what is libidinally the most important function of his body (urination) and in the *spatial arrangement* of the toys he expresses narrowness and the feeling of being caged, which we are inclined to trace to the early traumatic experience of being tied and to connect with his present fears of open spaces.

The boy then begins to ask persistently for many details about things in my room. When asked, "What is it you really want to know?", he quiets down quickly and in a dreamy way turns a shallow bowl upside down and puts many marbles into the cavity of its hollow base. This he repeats several times, then takes one toy car after the other, turns it upside down and examines it.

Here, finally, we have behavior which belongs to the "putting-into" and "taking-out" type of play. By his persistent questions, and his silent examination of the toy cars, he seems to express an intellectual problem: "What is the nature of the underside of things?" This question arises because of the real conflict with the objective world which began when his mother gave birth to his sister, and represents the material most accessible for future psychoanalytic interpretation.

Beneath this level we see that two aspects of his "physical" experiences are expressed in his play. The one indicating strong interest in a pregenital (urethral) function will, during treatment, offer material for interpretation and will at the same time necessitate retraining. The earlier experience, the feeling of being caged, seems to be connected deeply with the impression which a seemingly hostile world has made on this child when it was still so young that its only method of defense was a general withdrawal. This must have so influenced his whole mode of existence as to create severe resistances to the analytical or educational approach.

The crux of this resistance is shown in the fact that for an abnormally long time A wanted to walk only in a walker. To be tied, once distasteful, proved in this instance to be a protection. We may assume that it is this double aspect of physical restriction, what it once did to his ego and how his ego is now using it which A expressed in his very first play constructions when he was brought to me, because of his fear of openness and height.

2.

In stating that A expressed some quality of his experience of body and environment in the form of a cage-house, we imply not only that alloplastic behavior may reproduce the pattern of a traumatic impression and an autoplastic change imposed by it, but also that in play a house-form in particular may represent the body as a whole. And indeed, we read of dreams that: "The only typical, that is to say, regularly occurring representation of the human form as a whole is that of a house, as was recognized by Scherner." [1] As is well known, the same representation of the body by the image of a house is found throughout the gamut of human imagination and expression, in poetic fantasy, in slang, wit and burlesque, and in primitive language.

It would not, therefore, be important to lay much stress on the fact that in play, as well, a house-form can mean the body were it not that it is simple to ask a child to build a house, which often reveals the child's specific conception of and feeling for his own body and certain other bodies. We seem to have here a direct approach through play to the traces of those early experiences which formed his body-ego.

This assumption led to interesting results when older children and even adults were given the task of constructing a house. Two extreme examples may suffice here.

A girl of twelve, B, had, at the age of five, developed a severe neurosis following the departure of her first nurse, who had been in the house from the time of the child's birth. The nurse had spoiled B; for example, by allowing her to suck her thumb behind her mother's back, and to eat freely between meals. During the mother's frequent absences, B and her nurse lived in a world of their own standards; the nurse shared the secret of the girl's first sex play with a little boy, while the girl was the first person to hear of it when the nurse became pregnant. B had just begun to puzzle about this fact when the parents discovered it and peremptorily discharged the nurse. Knowing nothing of the shared secrets, they were unaware that in so doing they were suddenly depriving the girl of a queer and asocial intimacy for which she was unable

[1] Freud: *Introductory Lectures on Psychoanalysis*. London, Allen & Unwin, 1922, p. 128.

to find a substitute, especially since the mother set out to break in the shortest possible time, all of the bad habits left from the nurse's era. The result was a severe neurosis. When I saw the child for the first time with no knowledge of the psychogenesis of her neurosis, I noted a protruding abdomen, and my first impression was, "She walks like a pregnant woman". The secrets she had shared with her nurse and their pathogenic importance became apparent only later, however, when she confided that sometimes she heard voices within herself. One voice repeated: "Don't say anything, don't say anything", while others in a foreign language seemed to object to this command. She could save herself from the anxiety and the voices only by going into the kitchen and staying with the cook, obviously the person best fitted to represent the former nurse.

B first built a house without doors with a kind of annex containing a little girl doll (Figure 2a). Then she changed the house and built form 2b with many significant objects placed in and around it. In a vertical position we can see that the house-form could represent not only her own unusual posture but also the unconscious determinants for it, especially her identification with the pregnant nurse. The following superficial parallels (and I assume that deeper investigation of

FIGURE 2a

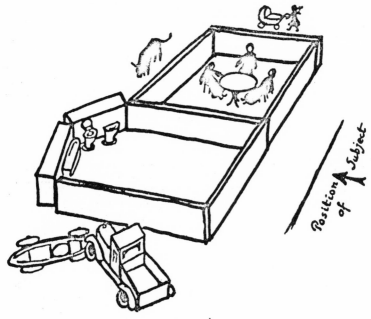

FIGURE 2*b*

similar cases would reveal these as typical spatial elaborations of infantile body feelings) may be drawn:

CONSTRUCTION	HOUSE	BODY
(1) A little girl with a baby carriage goes to the country (to the cow).	*Outside the House:* Where there is freedom.	*Head:* Where she thinks she would like to go away: to the nurse who gave her everything to eat.
(2) A family around a table.	*In the Dining Room:* Where the child has conflicts with the parents about eating. Where she is present when the parents (immigrants) talk about her in a foreign language.	*Inside the Body:* Where one feels conflicts. Where she hears foreign voices quarrel.
(3) A cow in the country.	*Outside the House.*	*In Front of the Chest:* Where women (nurses) have breasts which give milk.

CONSTRUCTION	HOUSE	BODY
(4) Bathroom furniture behind thick protruding walls.	*In the Bathroom* (thick walls) : Where the secret is (the closed doors); the forbidden (nakedness, masturbation); the dangers (threats concerning masturbation); the bloody things (menstruation) ; the dirty (toilet activities).	*In the Protruded Abdomen:* Where the secret is (the baby and its origin); that which is forbidden (the baby); the dangers (the growing baby); dirt (fæces).
(5) A red racer and a truck in collision.	*Outside the House:* Where the dangerous but fascinating life is, from which the parents try to protect the child. The accident.	*Under the Abdomen:* Where it seems a girl can lose something, since boys have something there and girls do not. Where people say girls will bleed. Where men do something to women. Where babies come out, hurt women and sometimes kill them (the nurse died shortly after childbirth).

3.

The doorless house not only pictures the child's posture, and snows the unconscious idea of having incorporated the lost nurse, it seems also to indicate that part of her body which is firmly entrenched within the fortress of ego-feelings, as distinguished from what are only thoughts and fears concerning the body, felt as "outside": the expectation of breasts and the fear of menstruation, of which she had been warned.

As a further example justifying our looking at the house from different positions and our assumption that the walls reveal something of the builder's body-ego, the following is of interest: A young schizophrenic man, C, a patient in the Worcester State Hospital, built the house shown in Figure 3.

He said it was a screen house all around, except for the back part. This patient complains of having no feeling in the front of his body. Ever since he was the "victim" of a spinal injection, he claimed that he suffered from a certain electric feeling drawing down from his spine to the rectum, and from difficulties in urination. He walked in a feminine manner with protruding buttocks. One may recognize this posture in the house-form. C strengthened that part of his house which corresponded to the spine of his body by placing two blocks on top of one another, and he furthermore placed walls around

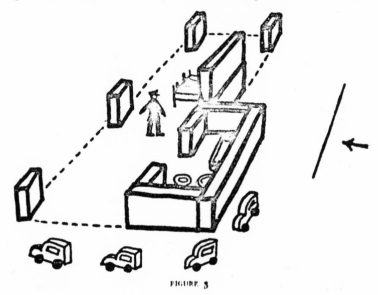

FIGURE 5

one room only (the bathroom) which in position corresponded to his buttocks. The cars are again put at the place corresponding to that of the urethro-genital region on the body and their arrangements suggested a symbolizing of the patient's urethral symptoms (he could urinate only "in bits").

In children without marked orality and adults without psychotic symptomatology, I have not found such detailed parallels between posture and house-forms as those of cases B and C. In laying out the plan of their houses, they stood over it in such a way that the house, as compared with a body, was "dorsal recumbent", and therefore might be said to represent more a baby's than an adult's body ego. By rotating the diagrams, we recognized in the same constructions the subject's posture which could be interpreted as expressing an identification with a mother image. It seems that the phenomenon of most striking similarity between house-forms and posture is based on the introjective and projective mechanisms of orality, which must be assumed to be active in the establishment of the body-ego in earliest childhood.

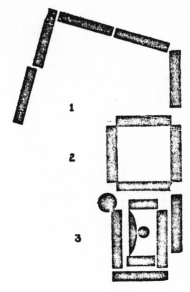

FIGURE 4

In attempting to find similar relationships between the growing organism and the typical block-building of normal children, one will have to be prepared for a much less striking and more sophisticated spatial language in which more emphasis is laid on structural principles than on similarity of shape. Interestingly enough, from Ruth Washburn's nonclinical material, only children with strongly emphasized orality produced parallels between body and house at all similar to B's and C's constructions. The house-form shown in Figure 4 was built by D, who was a fat, egoistic boy of five, a heavy eater. He explained that room 1 is the entrance, room 2 the living room. About room 3 he said: "This is where the water goes through; it is not going through now, though." He added, "There is a drawbridge; when boats come you pull it up." D's eagerness to "take in" and his reluctance "to give away" is well illustrated by the large opening of the entrance and the complicated closing arrangements at the other end, where water and boats go through the house.

4.

Returning to analytical material from children, we select a house-form of a boy of eight, E, which, in its primitiveness

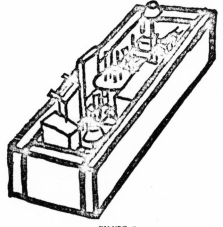

FIGURE 5

reminds us of A's construction. Upon my advice, E had been brought home from a special school where, diagnosed as defective, he had spent half his life. The problem was to find out whether with psychoanalytic help he could resume ordinary home and school life. When he came to his first hour, tense and hyperactive, he remained in my office just long enough to build a house with the blocks he found there (Figure 5). This house, primitive and without doors (like A's house), was filled chaotically with furniture. When, after a few minutes, he ran away shouting that he never would come back, he left behind him nothing but this doorless wall, dividing an outside from a chaotic inside.

I accepted this theme of a closed room and devoted the next few appointments to a short discussion of whether he had to stay and for how long, and whether or not the door of my room would remain open. On the second day he did not want to stay, although the door was not closed. He was immediately dismissed, sooner in fact than he really wanted to go. On the third day he stayed for a few minutes; on the fourth, he asked whether he could stay the whole hour; but when the door was closed, he was driven at once to manifestations of anxiety. He had to touch all the little buttons or protrusions in the room. I made the remark that it seemed as though he had to touch everything, and that he gave me somewhat the impression that for touching something (I did not know what) he expected to be put in jail. His blushing showed that he understood. Like most children who do not quite understand why they are detained with problem children, he had associated the sexual acts of some of them with his own sins and with "being a problem" in general. What he did not remember was that in his infancy, he, like A, had been tied when he rocked his bed (muscular masturbation with genital and anal elements).

The next day he asked questions, all of which began with, "Who has the power to . . ." and since I had heard from his mother that at home he was greatly worried because she wanted to get rid of a soiling cat, I told him that his mother had asked me about the cat and that I had told her she had no right to send the cat away. One should give cats and children a chance before one tries to get rid of them. He sat down and asked softly, "Why do I get so furious?"—and after a long silence, "Why do *boys* get so furious?" To every reader of Anna Freud's Introduction to Child Analysis it is obvious that this question shows a concern which is important for the therapeutic situation. While his defiant behavior at first had announced that he did not wish to be sent away or kept anywhere because of his violent aggression, his question showed insight, confidence and a readiness for conversation. I asked him why he thought boys were "furious". "Maybe because they are hunters . . .", he suggested.

Then we began to compare what boys wanted to be with what girls wanted to be, and to make out a written list containing on the one side the toys which boys liked: (streamline train, speedboat, gun, bow and arrow); and on the other those preferred by girls: (doll, doll's house, doll clothes, carriage, basket). The one group could be summed up under the symbol of an arrow and the other under that of a circle. I asked him whether this did not remind him of a certain detail in the difference between a boy's body and a girl's body. "That is why," he said thoughtfully, "I call my streamline train 'Johnny Jump-up'." So we talked about the psychobiological implications of having a penis, the fear of the impulses connected with its possession and the fear of the possibility of not having one. He seemed somewhat relieved.

The next day the cat interfered again. Her regression as to toilet habits had, to say the least, been overdetermined: she was, as everybody at home now agreed, pregnant. But no one could tell just when the kittens would arrive. The question, *when* do the kittens *want* to come out and *when* will they be *allowed* to come out, became the patient's main interest in life. Unfortunately, his unlucky father and his even more unlucky analyst happened to tell him different periods for the duration of a cat's pregnancy. He wondered seriously if God himself was sure when the kittens should come out.

One day, having left the office for a moment, I returned to find E all rolled up in the cover on the couch. He remained there half an hour. Finally, he crawled out and sat beside me. I began to talk about the kittens kept in the cat, children kept in special schools, babies tied in their beds and stillborn babies kept in glass jars. (I knew that not long ago he had seen such an exhibit, and that someone had jokingly told him it was actually a stillborn brother of his.) He probably could not remember, so I added that when he was a baby his father had tied him to his bed because he had rocked so loudly during the night. He blushed and when he got up from the sofa I noticed that he had tied his hands and feet before rolling himself up in the cover.

The toy which he subsequently chose for his first concentrated play in my office was a bowl (Figure 6), a piece of which was broken off. (It will be mentioned here in connection with several cases.) He turned it around to "shoot" marbles into it. For a while we competed at this game, until another cloud came up over the horizon.

FIGURE 6

As to Figure 5, one can see now how many different phenomena it "meant", all of them similar only in the possession of strong walls, no doors and chaos within—attributes at one and the same time of his tension of mind and body; his experience of being tied in bed; his concept of the female body as a claustrum; his experience and expectation of being kept at a place far from his family; and last, but not least, my office. In beginning our relationship with the "spatial" discussion of this last mentioned "cage" (office), we succeeded in lining up all his cage-conceptions before an interpretation which included them all was given. The play with the marbles, then, was the first free, though not yet quite uncompulsive, expression of that phallic tendency which, in its unsublimated form, had given him the impulse "to do something to women"—and the fear of "being put in jail". Soon afterwards his intrusive tendencies began to possess him entirely in the sublimated form of "scientific" curiosity. Appealing for comradely help from his father, and equipped with an extensible telescope, he entered Mother Nature's secluded areas and investigated birds' nests and other secrets.

5.

In analyzing the full significance of a certain house-form in play, as in the evaluation of a well-known dream symbol, we need the aid of biographical material. On the other hand, the form of the house itself and the play activity provoked by it, will sometimes tell at once where on the scale of object-relationships our small patient can be assumed to be; whether absorbed in narcissistic orality like B, C and D, or restricted by an early psychophysiological experience like A and E, or whether he has achieved a fearless, clear object-relationship, expressed in unrestricted functional play as in the case of F, which follows.

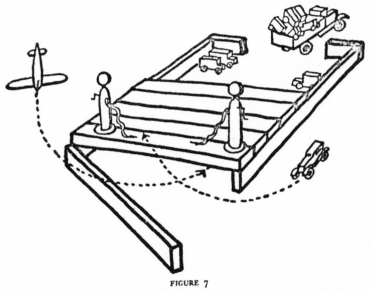

FIGURE 7

F, a boy of five, was not a patient—he was occasionally brought into the office to play for an hour (a pleasant procedure of regular, preventive observation). At the time of the visit to which I am referring, F talked at home in a rather unrepressed way about impulses towards his mother's body. She would, he hoped, let him put the next baby into her.

In my office he built a house (Figure 7), and played contentedly, without showing compulsion or anxiety, for a whole hour. Trucks drove into the backyard to unload dozens of little cars which were lined up. A little silver airplane and a red car were the favorites, and had individual rights: when the airplane majestically neared the house, the front door was opened to permit it to glide right in. The red car sometimes jumped on to the roof, to be fed by one of the two gasoline tanks stationed there. His remarks at home and his interest in his parents' bodies (so usual for this inquisitive age) justifies the interpretation that F played with the house as his fantasies played around his mother's body. The little red car is fed by the two tanks just as F's sister drinks from the mother's breasts. The airplane enters the house from the front as his father's erect penis enters the mother's body. And his loading and unloading of trucks indicates that like most children he has concluded that there are innumerable babies in the mother's body and that they are born through the rectum, the orifice through which the contents of his own body pass.

One was reminded of Santayana's recent description: "A boy at the age of five has a twentieth century mind; he wants something with springs and stops to be controlled by his little master-ego, so that the immense foreign force may seem all his own, and may carry him sky-high. For such a child, or such an adventurous mechanic, a mere shape or material fetish, like a doll, will never do; his pets and toys must be living things, obedient, responsive forces to be coaxed and led, and to offer a constant challenge to a constant victory. His instinct is masculine, perhaps a premonition of woman: yet he is not thinking of woman. Indeed, his women may refuse to satisfy his instinct for domination, because they share it; machines can be more exactly and more prodigiously obedient." [1]

II.

PSYCHOANALYSIS WITHOUT WORDS

(Abstract of a Case-history)

A little girl, G, two and one-half years old, had stopped looking and smiling at people and had ceased developing in her play. She had not learned to say a word or to communicate in any way with other children. Only occasionally, and then

[1] Santayana, George: *The Last Puritan*, New York: Charles Scribner's Sons, 1936, pp. 98–99.

in connection with some tense, compulsively repeated play, did her pretty face lose its monotonous and melancholy expression. At such moments her excited sounds were strangely guttural and were produced by noisy inhalations. No diagnosis meant much at this stage. The question was: Could one make contact with her at all? Could one reawaken her interest in this world?

Upon my first visit to her, one single fact induced me to make the trial. As she approached me slowly, coming down a stairway, she did not look at me directly but around me in concentric circles. She did not fail to see me, as had been supposed, but definitely avoided doing so.

My first subsequent observations revealed that her spells of excitement showed a mixture of pleasure and anxiety. I noticed this first during a spell which took place as she was banging a door, which in opening and closing touched a small chain that hung from an electric light. However, such "spells" could also occur when she was quiet. She would suddenly look out of the corners of her eyes at an extreme angle, focusing them far away, usually at the brightest point in the surroundings; then she would twist her hands almost convulsively and produce guttural sounds, half like crying, half laughing.

She seemed never to have made any of the usual pre-language sounds: nor had she ever licked things as other children do, nor bitten anything. She would urinate only once in twelve or twenty-four hours, and often had bowel movements only once in forty-eight hours. Her room was overclean and her nurse seemed not without anxiety in regard to these matters.

When I heard this, and saw her exhibit the same excitement while simply throwing a ball again and again between a piano stool and a piano, I concluded that she had experienced training as a trauma, which in turn had been connected somehow with unknown traumata of her earlier life. I first tried to approach this symptom by suggestive play. Disregarding her, since she avoided looking at me, I threw stones into some old "potties" for almost an hour. When I then left, and observed her from a place where she could not see me, she played around these potties in concentric circles which grew narrower and narrower. Finally she dropped a stone in a potty, laughed heartily and loudly, and said clearly, "a-ba-ba-ba-ba". During the succeeding days her toilet habits changed completely, whether as a result of this simple suggestion I do not know, but an immediate relief of general tension was obvious.

We then tried by mild suggestion to influence her playing and her playful movements in space. She had not only fortified her position against the outer world by not looking at people, not listening, not eating unfamiliar food, and by holding back urine and fæces, but she behaved on the whole as if something actually inhibited the movements of her body in space. Her legs and arms were tense and stiff, so much so that a neurological disturbance was suspected and she was examined, with no findings to indicate disease. Even when ample space was at her disposal, she seemed to imagine limits and boundaries where she stopped suddenly, as if confronted with a fence or an abyss. It was an imaginary noise at a certain distance upon which she then focused her attention with an expression half anxious, half delighted. I was interested to see at what limit freer play and freer physical movement would be stopped by a real anxiety or end in the manifest excitement described above. If she threw things, I would try to induce her to throw them further; I would take her hand to run with her, to jump down or to climb steps—always somewhat more quickly or extensively than she would dare to do alone.

While attempting to help her expand the limits of her expression, it became obvious that there was a correlation between the functions of focusing on objects, grasping objects, aiming at things, biting into things, forming sounds, having sufficiently large bowel movements, and touching her genitals. The manifestation of increasing aggressiveness in one of these functions was accompanied by similar improvements in the others; but when a certain limit was reached, anxiety inhibited all of them. A sudden large defæcation on the porch was followed by severe constipation and regression in all functions, and a "talking" spell of four hours one night, in which she seemed to be able to talk all the languages of Babel, but unable to single out English from the confusion, had the same effect.

The first word she suddenly used—pronouncing it quite clearly—showed that it had been right to assume an early traumatic experience. While banging a door she looked far away into the sky and exclaimed (obviously imitating an anxious adult, quite in the fashion of a parrot), "Oh dear, oh dear, oh dear." On another occasion, she said clearly several times, "My goodness". A few days later I saw her pick out of a potty numerous stones and blocks which smelled of paint, and lick them. When I softly said, "Oh dear, oh dear", she vigorously threw the potty away, as if remembering a prohibition.

On the other hand, nothing could excite her more than having a bright, shining pinwheel moved quickly toward her face. I cannot report here all of the details of her play, which finally pointed to the following elements as possible aspects of a traumatic situation in her past: looking through bars (like those of a crib?); a light moving quickly toward her face; a light seen at a certain angle; a light seen far away; traumatic interference with licking and with play somehow connected with defæcation. These corresponded to two of the definite fears she had occasionally manifested, i.e., of a light in the bathroom and of a traffic light blinking some hundred feet away from her window. She had also been terrified by the fringes of the covers on her parents' beds, a fear which seemed unconnected with this, until the chains of the lights which fascinated or frightened her proved to play an important rôle.

I then visited the hospital where she had been born. The most critical period of her short life had been its first few weeks, during which her mother had been too ill to nurse her for more than two days. The baby developed an almost fatal diarrhœa. Not much was known about this period and her special hospital nurse had left the country.

Another nurse, helping me to study the lights in the hospital, suddenly said, "And then we have another lamp which we only use with babies who have severe diarrhœa." She demonstrated the following procedure with its clear parallels to the child's play behavior. The baby is laid on its side so that the lamp, which is put as near as possible to the baby's sore buttocks, can shine directly on them. The baby then must see the lamp from approximately the angle which this child's eyes always assume when she is preoccupied with her typical day-dream. The lamp has a holder which can be bent and the full light could then shine on the baby's face for a moment as the lamp is being adjusted. When this has been done, the lamp is covered so that it is, so to speak, in the bed. For the baby, then, the *light is where the pain is.*

The discovery of this traumatic event from the second week of her life helped us to meet a situation which arose when the child suddenly became frightened of a lamp in my office, stopped drinking milk at home and began, wherever she was, to play at being in bed. She would build a kind of cave out of the cover of my couch, crawl into it, and terrified but fascinated, would look towards the dangerous light. We began to play with lights. Since at that time she liked all things which could be spun around quickly, I would put a light underneath the cover, presumably where the hospital lamp had been, and would spin it around. She began to love lights, and when she smiled for the first time at the light that she had been afraid of, she said, "ma-ma-ma-ma". At the same time her motor coördination improved so much that when the lamp above her bed had to be unscrewed because she played with it too much she could rock her bed across the room in the dark to pull another lamp chain.

At this point in the treatment the mother remembered another important part of the child's earliest history. In the third month of the child's life, when she had left the girl to take a trip, she had given instructions that an electric heater be turned on while diapers were being changed. After her return she was told that all through this month, dynamite had been used to blast rocks in the vicinity and had terrified the whole neighborhood. The baby, being upset already by the nervousness of the adults, had been further terrified when one day the electric heater suddenly exploded beside her. Here we have the connection between *the light where the pain is* and *the light where the noise is*. The flashing traffic light several hundred feet away, of which she consequently was afraid, apparently was a "condensation" of the exploding light near at hand and the terrifying noises at a distance.

After she had learned to play with lights without fear, we attempted to extend further the radius of her activities, and gave her hard toast in order to induce her to bite. She refused —and presently reacted with a show of fear on seeing a tassel hanging from the girdle of her mother's dress. At the same time, she began to bite into wooden objects. Having observed in her a similar fear of a lamp chain (usually, as I pointed out, the object of traumatic play) directly after she had first seen two little boys naked, I inquired whether, and how much, she could have seen of her father's and mother's bodies. Her fear spread to all objects which had tassels or fringes or were furry or hairy, when they were worn by a person. When offered her mother's belt to play with, she touched and finally took it between thumb and forefinger as if she were taking a living and detestable thing, and threw it away (with an expression much like that occasionally shown by women when they report a snake dream). When by playing with the fringe repeatedly, she had overcome her fear of it, she began staring down into the neck of her mother's nightgown, focusing her fascinated attention on her breasts. When we add to these observations the recollection of how she had formerly looked in a concentric circle around people, supposedly not seeing anybody at all, we may reconstruct one more of the traumatic impressions which were probably factors in arresting her development. We may assume that as a small child when seeing her parents undressing on a beach, she had experienced a biting impulse toward the mother's breasts and (a not uncommon displacement) the father's penis.[1] What this meant to her becomes clear when we remember the first two traumatic events we were able to uncover. The first had been the experience of intestinal and

---

[1] As to the developmental relationship of biting and focusing, see Chapter III, B.

anal pain in association with light during the frustrated sucking period.   The second was the experience of noise (the
blasting) and exclaiming women ("Oh dear," "My goodness")
in connection with the electric heater during the onset of the
biting period.   (Other material suggested that the nurse had
exclaimed in a similar way when she once found the child
playing with fæces which she was about to put into her mouth.)

No doubt from the very outset this child had not been ready
to master stimulations above a certain intensity.   On the other
hand, some meaning could be detected in her strange behavior
and, under the influence of our play and of a simultaneous
change of atmosphere in a now more enlightened environment,
the child's vocalizations approached more nearly the babble of
a normal child before it speaks.   She began to play happily
and untiringly with her parents and to enjoy the presence of
other children.   She had fewer fears, and she developed skills.
This newly acquired relationship to the object world, though
a precondition of any reorientation, was, of course, only a
beginning.

III.

PREGENITALITY AND PLAY

A. Clinical Observations

1.

In her article, *Ein Fall von Essstörung* [1], Editha Sterba reports
the case of a little girl who began to hold food in her mouth,
after having been trained to release the fæces which for an
annoyingly long period she had preferred to retain in her rectum.   This food she would turn around and around until it
formed a ball, whereupon she would spit it out, thus using
or rather misusing, the mouth to execute an act which had
been inhibited at the anus.

A zone of the body with a specific muscular and nervous
structure, the typical function of which is to accept, examine
and prepare an incoming object for delivery to the inside of

[1] Ztschr. f. psa. Pädagogik IX, 1935.

the body, is here used instead to hold for a while in a playful manner, and then return the object to the outside. This act resembles the anal act which it replaces only as a "gesture", but without any functional logic. Such an "unnatural" use of a substituted zone is one form of what is called *displacement*. In this case it implies a partial regression, since the mouth precedes the anus in the erogenous zones sequence, and offers the specific tactual pleasure sought after at an earlier period. It is hard to understand psycho-physiologically that a zone can replace another zone of different neurological quality and location, and serve dramatically to represent its function. Psycho-analysts have accepted the interrelationship of these interchangeable zone-phenomena as being libido economical. Physiologists and psychologists in general are for the most part not even aware of the phenomena as a problem.

What interests us most in this connection is the relationship to play of such displacements from one organ to another. Most children instead of displacing from one section of their own body to another, find objects in the toy world for their extra-bodily displacements. If, in a moment of deep concentration in play, the dynamics of which are yet to be described, a child is not disturbed from within or without, he may use a cavity in a toy as a representative of a cavity in his own body, thus externalizing the entire dynamic relationship between the zone and its object.

Between displacements within the body (habits, symptoms) and the free external displacement in play, we find various arresting combinations. A little boy, H, two-and-one-half years of age, who struggled rather belatedly against enuresis, began to take to bed with him little boxes, which he held closed with both hands. When a box would open during the night, sometimes apparently with his unconscious help, he would cry out in his sleep, or awaken and call for someone to help him close the box. Then he would sleep peacefully, though not necessarily dry. But he continued to experiment. During the day he looked around for suitable boxes—obviously driven by an urge to materialize an image of "closedness".

Finally he found what seemed to fit the image: it was a cardboard cylinder which had been the center of a roll of toilet paper, and two cardboard caps from milk bottles, which he put over the openings of the roll. (See Figure 8.) All through the

FIGURE 8

night he would try to hold this arrangement firmly together with both hands—as an animistic guardian of the retentive mode. But no sooner had his training achieved a relative success in closing his body during sleep, then he began, *before* going to sleep, to throw all available objects out of the window. When this was made impossible, he stole into other rooms and spilled the contents of boxes and bottles on the floor.

Clearly, the first act, namely, holding a closed box as a necessary condition for sleep, resembles a compulsive act originating in the child's fear of being overpowered by his weakness to retain or his wish to expel. Emptying objects, on the other hand, or throwing them out of the window is "delinquent" and the result of the fear of being overpowered by the claims of *society to which he surrenders the zone but not the impulse*. The impulse begins an independent existence.

To prevent the little boy from throwing things out of the window, it was opened from the top. Thereupon he was found riding on it, leaning out into the night. I do not think he would have fallen out; he wanted only to show himself "master of openings", as compensation for the surrender of the free use of his excretory openings to society. When, in consequence, his mother kept his window closed until he was asleep, he insisted that the door should be ajar. At an earlier stage, the same boy, as he was learning to control his bowel movements had gone through a short period of excessive running away. Thus not only sections of one's body and toys, but also the body as a whole in its spatial relationship to the whole room or to the whole house may serve the displaced impulse in various degrees of compulsive, naughty, or playful acts.

I may refer again to the wooden bowl, which I mentioned in note 1 (see Figure 6). After a piece had been broken off, this bowl proved to be of manifold use to various children. They used it with deep concentration and with endless repetitions. As noted in Chapter I, A, curious and much restricted, turned it upside down to fill its hollow base and look at it; F, reassured about his phallic aggressiveness, used the opening, as thousands of boys at certain ages do, as a goal for his marbles; G, over-retentive, did not "retain" marbles in the bowl, but filled it again and again in order to spill them excitedly all over the floor. Similarly, a girl of three, who was fighting desperately against soiling herself, did not spill, but asked for the broken-off piece to close the bowl tightly, reminding us of the boy H with his animistic retention boxes. Thus we see the impulses appearing in play as the advance guard or rear guard of new sublimations.

It is conceivable that a form such as this bowl, as it is used by children of various age groups, could also prove of experimental value. We must keep in mind, however, that units of play behavior, like parts of dreams or single associations, seldom have independent meaning value. To know what a certain configuration in a child's play means, we should know the contemporaneous changes in his growth, his habits, his character and his concepts of others.

2.

Let us look at an individual who showed pathological oscillation in the pregenital sphere, and let us place a specific bit of play in the center of our observational field.

At a certain period in his treatment, J, a boy of eight, untiringly repeated the following play: A caterpillar tractor slowly approached the rear end of a truck, the door of which had been opened. A dog had been placed on the tractor's chain wheels in such a way that he was hurled into the truck at the moment the tractor bumped into it. (Figure 9.)

Symptom. In a very specific way, J had failed to respond to toilet training. Dry and clean when he wished to be, he had nevertheless continued to express resistance against his mother by frequent soiling (as much as three times a day), an act which became a perverted expression of his highly ambivalent feelings about the other sex. In school, when angered by certain girls by whom he would feel seduced, he would take their

FIGURE 9

berets to the toilet and defæcate into them. His masturbatory habit consisted in rubbing the lower part of his abdomen, which caused genital excitement at first, but ended in defæcation.

First treatment. The psychiatrist who first treated the boy was amazed to find that he offered "unconscious" material of a sexual and anal nature in a never ending stream. As the naïve preconception in some child guidance clinics would express it, the boy was a real "freudian" patient. But the psychiatrist was well aware of the fact that the patient did not really respond to the explanations for which he seemed to ask. This was probably due to the fact that in being voluble he did not communicate with the therapeutic agency in order to get cured, but cleverly "backed out" by regressing to a new kind of oral perversion in "talking about dirty things".

Second treatment. When the boy's masturbation increased,

it had been thought necessary to circumcise him, assuming that it was a slight phimosis which though stimulating him geni-tally, did not allow him to have a full erection and led his excitement into anal-erotic channels. Simultaneously, he was subjected to an encephalogram. Following this, the boy had stopped soiling entirely: but he also underwent a complete character change. He talked little, looked pale, and his intel-ligence seemed to regress—symptoms which are apt to be over-looked for some time because of the specific improvement in regard to a socially more annoying symptom. In this case, the closing up was nothing but a further regression, an outwardly more convenient, but in fact more dangerous retreat into orality (as was also shown by his excessive eating) and into a generaliza-tion of the retentive impulse. In consequence, his behavior soon gave rise to grave concern, and when he was first referred to me, I was doubtful as to the therapeutic reliability of his ego which seemed to be either no longer, or perhaps never to have been, secure.

Psychoanalytic treatment. The first barrier which psycho-analysis was forced to attack was the castration fear, which, after the circumcision, had suppressed his soiling without rid-ding him of the impulse. Expecting new physical deprivations, the boy would appear equipped with two pairs of eyeglasses on his nose, three knives on a chain hanging out of his trousers and a half dozen pencils sticking out of his vest pocket. Alter-nately he was a "bad guy" or a cross policeman. He would settle down to quiet play only for a few moments, during which he would choose little objects (houses, trees and people) no larger than two or three inches high, and make covers for them out of red plasticene. Suddenly he would get very pale and ask for permission to go to the bathroom. When consequently the circumcision was talked over and reassurances given for the more important remainder of his genitals, his play and co-operation became more steady.

His first drawing pictured a woman with some forms en-larged so as to represent large buttocks. In violent streaks he covered her with brown paint. It was not, however, until his castration fear had been traced to earlier experiences, that he began to look better and to play with real contentment.

J had witnessed an automobile accident in which the chief damage was a flat tire. In describing this and similar incidents to me he almost fainted, as he had also done merely while enlarging and protecting the little toys with covers of plasticene. In view of his anxiety, I pressed this point. He felt equally sick when I asked him about certain sleeping arrangements. It appeared that he had seen (in crowded quarters) a man perform intercourse with a woman who sat on him, and he had observed that the man's penis looked shorter afterwards. His first impression had been that the woman, whose face seemed flushed, had defæcated into the man's umbilicus and had done some harm to his genitals. On second thought, however, he associated what he had seen with his observations on dogs, concluding that the man had, as it were, eliminated a part of his penis into the woman's rectum out of which she later would deliver, i.e., again eliminate, the baby. His castration fear was traced to this experience, and the enlightenment given that semen and not a part of the penis remained in the woman.

First play. His first concentrated skilful and sustained play was with the tractor and the truck. At that moment I made no interpretation of it to him, but to me it indicated that he wanted to make sure by experimenting with his toys that the pleasant idea of something being thrown into another body without hurting either the giver or the receiver was sensible and workable. At the same time, his eliminative as well as his intrusive impulses helped him in arranging the experiment. Finally he showed that his unresolved anal fixation (no doubt in coöperation with certain common "animalistic" tendencies and observations) did not allow him to conceive of intrusion in any other way than from behind. From his smearing of the woman's picture with brown paint to this game, he had advanced one step: it was not as before brown stuff or mud which was thrown into the truck, it was something living.

Technical consideration. Melanie Klein, in her arresting and disturbing book, The Psychoanalysis of Children, has given the significance of an independent, symbolical unit to the fact that in a child's play motor cars may represent human bodies doing something to one another. Whether or not this is unreservedly true in its exclusively sexual interpretation has become a matter of controversy. Probably the question cannot be given any stereotyped answer. Symbolism is dangerous because it distracts attention from the imponderables of interpretation. No doubt, any group of mechanical objects, such as radiators, elevators, toilet and water systems, motor cars, and so on, which are inanimate but make strange noises, have openings to incorporate, to retain and to eliminate, and finally are able to move rapidly and recklessly, constitute a world well suited to symbolize one of the early concepts which the child has of his body as he develops the agencies of self-observation and self-criticism. Encountering in himself a system of incalculable and truly "unspeakable" forces, the child seeks a counterpart for his inner experience in the unverbalized world of mechanisms and mute organisms. As projections of a being which is absorbed in the experiences of growth, differentiation, and objectivation, they are not as yet systematically described. Their psychological importance certainly goes beyond sexual symbolism in its narrower sense.

Likewise, play is much too basic a function in human and animal life to be regarded merely as an infantile substitute for the verbal manifestations of an adult. Therefore one cannot offer any stereotyped advice as to the form or time when interpretations of play are to be given to a child. This will depend entirely on the rôle of play at the specific age and in the specific stage of each child patient. In general, a child who is playing with concentration should be left undisturbed as long as his own anxiety allows him to develop his ideas—but no longer. On the other hand, some children becoming aware of our interest in play, use this to lead us astray and away from quite conscious realities which should be verbalized. We are not in possession of a theory embracing the dynamics of play

and verbalization for different ages in childhood. We do not
want to make the child conscious of the fact that play as such
means something, but only that his fears, his inability to play
playfully, may mean something. In order to do this, it is
almost never advisable to show to the child that any one
element in his play "means" a certain factor in his life. It is
enough after one has drawn one's own conclusions from the
observation of play, to begin to talk with the child about the
critical point in his life situation—in a language the sense of
which is concrete to a child at a specific age. If one is on the
right track, the child's behavior (through certain positive and
negative attitudes not discussed here) will lead the way as far
as it is safe. No stereotyped imagery should lure us beyond
this point.

Return of the impulse. Outside the play hours, the eliminative impulse typically made its reappearance in J's life in
macrocosmic [1] fashion and at the periphery of the life space:
the whole house, the whole body, the whole world, was used
for the representation of an impulse which did not yet dare to
return to its zone of origin. In his sleep, he would start to
throw the belongings of other people, and only theirs, out of
the window. Then, in the daytime, he threw stones into
neighbors' houses and mud against passing cars. Soon he deposited fæces, well wrapped, on the porch of a hated woman
neighbor. When these acts were punished, he turned violently against himself. For days he would run away, coming
back covered with dirt, oblivious of time and space. He still
did not soil, but desperation and the need for elimination
became so all powerful that he seemed to eliminate *himself* by
wild walks without any goal, coming back so covered with mud
that it was clear he must have undressed and rolled in it.
Another time he rolled in poison ivy and became covered with
the rash.

Resistance. When he noticed that, by a slowly narrowing network of interpretations, I wanted to put into words those of

[1] See part 3 of this note.

his impulses which he feared most, namely, elimination and intrusion in their relationship to his mother, he grew pale and resistive. The day I told him that I had the impression there was much to say about his training at home, he began a four-day period of fæcal retention, stopped talking and playing, and stole excessively, hiding the objects. As all patients do, he felt rightly that verbalization means detachment and resignation: He did not dare to do the manifest, but he did not want to give up the latent.

Return of symptom. He did not live at home at this time. After many weeks, he received the first letter from his mother. Retiring to his room, he shrank physically and mentally, and soiled himself. For a while he did this regularly whenever his mother communicated with him.[1] It was then possible to interpret to him his ambivalent love for his mother, the problems of his bowel training, and his theories concerning his parents' bodies. It was here also that his first free flow of memories and associations appeared, allowing us to verbalize much that had been dangerous only because it had been amorphous. Interestingly enough, after the patient understood the whole significance of the eliminative problem in his life, the eliminative impulse, in returning to its zone did not flood, as it were, the other zones. Verbalization did not degenerate to "elimination of dirt" this time, as in the previous psychiatric treatment.

Sublimation. One day he suddenly expressed the wish to make a poem. If there ever was a child who, in his make-up and behavior, did not lead one to expect an æsthetic impulse, it was J.[2] Nevertheless, in a flood of words, produced during an excitement similar to that which had been noticeable when he had talked about dirt to the psychiatrist, he now began to dictate song after song about beautiful things. Then he proposed the idea, which he almost shrieked, of sending these poems to his mother. The act of producing and writing these

[1] In concluding a letter to his mother, J wrote instead of "Love, J", "Left, J."

[2] See, however, case P (Oriol) in Chapter IV.

poems, of putting them into envelopes and into the mailbox,
fascinated him for weeks.   He *gave* something to his mother
and it was *beautiful!*   The intense emotional interest in this
new medium of expression and the general change in habits
accompanying it, indicate that by means of this act of sending
something beautiful to his mother, part of that libido which
had participated in the acts of retaining fæces from women
and eliminating dirt to punish them had achieved sublimation.
The impulse had found a higher level of expression: the zone
submitted to training.

3.

In part 1 of this note, I gave an example of what different
children may do with one toy; in part 2, an example of the
therapeutic significance of one play-event in a child's life.   I
would like to add a word about a child's behavior with different play-media:

A child playing by himself may find amusement in the play
world of his own body—his fingers, his toes, his voice, constitut-
ing the periphery of a world which is self-sufficient in the
mutual enchantment of its parts.   Let us call this most primitive form of play *autocosmic.*   Gradually objects which are
close at hand are included, and their laws taken into account.

If, at another stage, the child weaves fantasies around the
reality of objects, he may construct a small toy world which is
dominated by the laws of his own growing body and mind:·
Thus, he makes blocks "grow" by placing them on top of one
another; and, with obvious pleasurable excitement in repetition
he knocks them down, thus externalizing the trauma of his own
falls.   Later the blocks may serve as the building stones for a
miniature world in which an ever increasing number of bodily,
mental and social experiences are externalized and dramatized.
This manifestation we may call *microcosmic play.*

We can term *macrocosmic* that form of play in which the
child moves as in a kind of trance among life-sized objects,
pretending that they are whatever background he needs for

his imagination. Thus he manifests his need for omnipotence in a material which all too often is rudely claimed by adults, because it has other, "grown-up" purposes.

These are a few of the more basic types of play which the child offers to us for comparison—each with its special kind of infantile fascination—developing one after the other as he grows and then shifting more or less freely from one to the other at certain stages.

Following an exceptional sequence of disappointments and frustrations, a girl of eight, K, a patient of Dr. Florence Clothier of Boston, made a veritable fortress of herself. Stubborn, stiff, uncommunicative, she would occasionally open all the orifices of her body, and annoy her environment by spitting, wetting, soiling, and passing flatus. One received the impression that these symptoms were not only animistic acts by which she eliminated hated intruders (her stepmother and her stepbrother), but also "shooting" with all available ammunition. While polymorphous in their zonal expression, these acts were clearly dominated by a combination of the eliminative and intrusive impulses. As the main object of the destructive part of this impulse, one could recognize the stepmother's body, in which the child suspected that more rival stepbrothers were growing. Naturally, this wild little girl was at the same time most anxious to find for herself a good mother's body in which to hide, to cry, and to sleep. Someone had told her that her own mother had died while giving birth to her; and one can imagine what conflicts arose when she first met the psychiatrist and saw that this potentially new and better mother was actually pregnant.

These biographic data are enough to explain the play which I am going to describe. Nevertheless, there is nothing essentially atypical in this play. This girl's constitution and experience simply made dominant the problem of intrusion which every child faces at least in one period of his life, namely, in the phallic period.

The phallic phase, last of the ambivalent stages, leads the

child into a maze of "claustrum" fantasies, in which some children—for a longer or shorter time—get hopelessly lost.[1] They want to touch, enter and know the secrets of all interiors but are frightened of dark rooms and dream of jails and tombs. As they flee the claustrum they would like to hide in mother's arms; fleeing their own disturbing impulses toward the mother's body they escape into wilful acts of displaced violence, only to be restricted and "jailed" again. The mother's body into which the baby wanted to retreat in order to find food, rest, sleep, and protection from the dangerous world, becomes in the phallic phase the dangerous world, the very object and symbol of aggressive conquest. Further obstructing this conquest are the father's rights (because of his strength) and the younger siblings' rights (because of their weakness); and thus the mother, a heaven and hell at the same time, becomes the center of a hopeless rivalry. Whether to go forward or backward, to be hero or baby,—that is the question. It is in this phase that the boy, knowing there is no way back, sets his face towards the future (where all those ideals are waiting for him, which we symbolize by superhuman mother figures); while to the girl, her own body's claustrum offers a vague promise and new dangers.

In his play, the boy at this stage prefers games of war and crime, and expresses most emphatically the intrusive mode; the girl, by contrast, in caring for dolls, in building a small house with a toy baby or a toy animal in it or in other protective configurations expresses the procreative-protective tendency which will remain the point of reference for whatever course she may take in her future.

Dr. Clothier's patient, in her play during a period of transition from eliminative-intrusive to female tendencies, showed many distorted manifestations of these problems:

In *cutting* her own hair and eyelashes, and threatening to cut her eyes and teeth, she approximated a return into the *autocosmic* sphere of play.

Microcosmic: (1) *Dramatic:* Five dolls, named after father,

[1] See case E.

stepmother, stepbrother, sister and herself are approached from behind by a *snake* who *eats* everybody except herself and her pet animal.

(2) *Pictorial:* Drawings with long rows of houses which are being approached, entered, and left by a *stealing* cat: The house more and more assumed the appearance of the human body, with the two sides of the walk leading to it representing the legs between which the door was entered by the cat. The girl noticed this resemblance herself and made the giggling remark, "Do you think that a house can stand on the walk?"

Macrocosmic: (1) For several days she built "houses". The entrance had two round portal forms represented by a dish on each side. The patient began going in and out of the house on all fours, always entering the house backwards. When inside, she picked up one of the dishes and pretended to drink from it; then she curled up in a fœtal position. Crawling backwards over and over again, she said to the psychiatrist, "You watch and tell me so I won't hit the back of the house." The psychiatrist told her when to stop, but each time she gave a vicious lunge backwards, *breaking* through the wall.

(2) Where her macrocosmic play expanded beyond the sphere of toys, i.e., became naughty, she climbed on tables, desks and shelves, *invaded* drawers, and *tore* papers. Often only bursting in and out of the room was an act big enough to express her intrusive rage.

(3) At a decisive point in her treatment, the girl was especially fascinated by a rubber syringe with which she *squirted water* everywhere. "Now I'm a wild Indian, so look out!" On a certain day, during a period of a general change in attitude, the girl squirted on the floor a big circle with one line representing a radius ⏀ ; then she angrily made a puddle out of her design. The next day she repeated the same configuration, but added a small circle in the center of the big one: ◉ On the third day, she again drew a larger circle and, without the connecting radius, a smaller circle in the center, saying, "This is a baby circle." ◎ This time she did not destroy the figure, but said giggling, "There are no cats

here" (to enter the circle and steal the baby). The change of configurations in this play from phallic (syringe) to female-protective is obvious. Moreover the little girl created a symbol and in doing so seemed to have a moment of clarity and pacification.

(4) Around the same time she dictated the following story to a teacher. She said she had heard it somewhere. We add it as an association which in a *narrative* and quite humorous form seemed to express symbolically an acceptance of the difference between boys and girls:

The Pumpkin and the Cat: The farmer put the pumpkin in the barn, and the cat came, and the cat said to the pumpkin, "Do you want to stay here? Let's go away." And the pumpkin rolled and tumbled, and the cat walked and walked, until it began to rain. The cat lifted up his wet paw. A woodcutter came by. The pumpkin said, "Mister, will you please cut my top off, and scrape all the seeds out, so the cat can come in?" The woodcutter cut off the top of the pumpkin and scraped all the seeds out.

They went on tumbling and rolling until morning. They started off again, tumbling and rolling. Then pretty soon it was night. And it began to rain harder, and the cat lifted up his wet paw, and the pumpkin said; "You'd better get inside." "Yes, but we haven't got any two windows and a nose and a mouth." The pumpkin said, "You get out and I'll go to the carpenter." He went to the carpenter and said, "Mr. Carpenter, will you please cut two windows and a nose and mouth?"

The cat came in the pumpkin and the pumpkin and the cat laughed. Then they rolled and tumbled, until they came to a little house. They heard a boy whistling and then a girl came out of the house and said, "What do you wish you had most for Halloween?" The boy said: "I wish I had a nice round pumpkin", and the girl said, "I wish I had a nice little black cat."

Up rolled the pumpkin to the little boy, and the girl said, "Look what the fairy brought us, and I think it's a cat inside!"

And off jumped the cover, and out jumped the little black cat, and right into the little girl's arms.

And they lighted the pumpkin, and put it on the table, and put the kitty next to it, until the mother came home.

B. Zones, Impulses, Modes

1.

It is not only in pathological cases that children's acts impress us as being unexpected and apparently incoherent. The observer of any child's life feels at moments that an essential factor is eluding him, as the loon in the lake eludes the hunter by sudden turns under the surface. Whether the child is playful, naughty or compulsive; whether his acts involve bodily functions or toys, persons or abstracts, only analytic comparison reveals that what so suddenly appears in one category is essentially related to that which disappeared in another. Sometimes it is the mere replacement in time which makes the analyst become aware of the inner connection of two acts; sometimes it is a quality of an emotion or a tendency of a drive common to both. Often, however, (and this is especially true for the period of pregenitality on which we focus our attention here) the only observational link between two acts is what we wish to describe as the organ-mode.[1]

To clear the way for more systematic observations of the interrelationship between the intrabodily and extrabodily aspects of pregenitality, it seems best to reduce the displaced impulses to the simplest spatial terms, i.e., to signs which represent the dynamic principle of the body apertures in which the impulses are first centered. I propose that we accept the sign   ⟳ as representing the incorporation of an object by means of *sucking*.   ⟳ may represent the incorporation by means of *biting*;   ◯ *the retaining of* or *closing up* against an object;   ◯ *expelling* and   ⟶ *intruding*.

[1] When the author first used the scheme to be presented on the following pages in order to explain certain play phenomena in a seminar in Boston, in 1934, he did not know of F. Alexander's "vector analysis". (See the publications of the Chicago Psychoanalytic Institute.) For the limited purpose of these notes, it seems better not to discuss Alexander's conclusions.

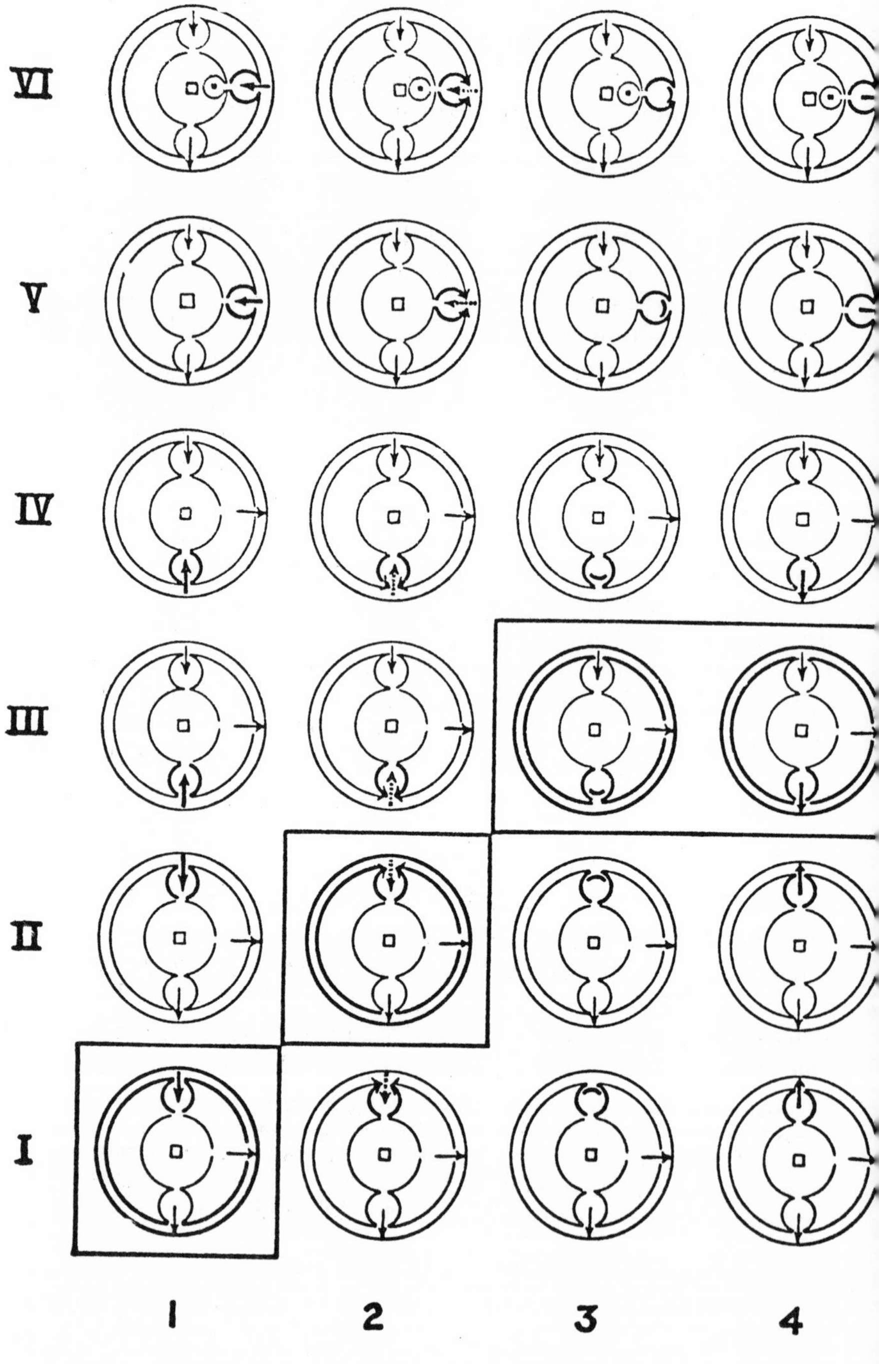
VI
V
IV
III
II
I
1
2
3
4

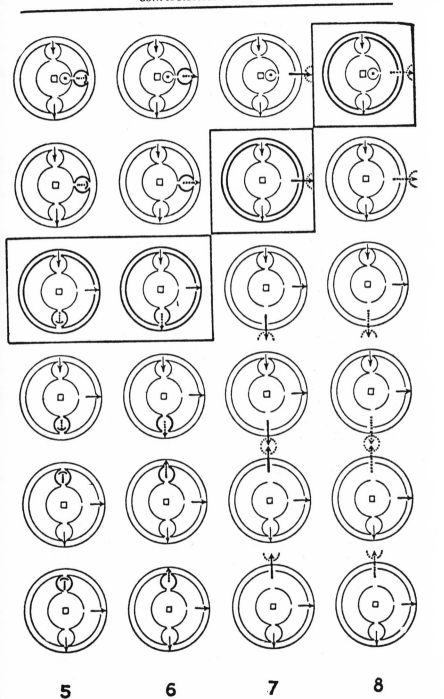

5   6   7   8

The organ-modes, then, are the common spatial modalities peculiar to the appearance of pregenital impulses throughout their range of manifestation: whether gratification is experienced in the elimination of waste product by a body aperture, by the spilling of a bottle's content, by throwing objects out of a window, or pushing a person out of one's physical sphere, we recognize the mode of elimination as the common descriptive characterization of all these acts, and conclude that we are confronted with interchangeable manifestations of what was originally the impulse of elimination.

Surveying the field of these manifestations, one finds that what Freud has described as pregenitality is the development through a succession of narcissistic organ cathexes of impulses which represent all the possible relationships of a body and an object. Pregenitality not only teaches all the patterns of emotional relationship, it also offers all the spatial modalities of experience. Led by pregenital impulses (or confused by them as the case may be) children experiment more or less playfully in space with all the possible relationships of one object to another one and of the body as a whole to space.

For didactic purposes, I have arranged the modes in a chart of pregenitality which (in a formulation without words) indicates the network of original interrelationships of zones and impulses. This chart has–been helpful in observation and teaching when used as a short-cut, leading to but by no means avoiding the knowledge of the other components of pregenitality.

Nobody who works in the field of human behavior can be unaware of the dangers of or blind to the necessity for such tentative systematization.

The chart is composed of single diagrams which represent the human organism in the successive stages of emphasis on certain erotogenic zones in pregenitality. I 1, for example, like all the other diagrams, consists of three concentric circles which represent three primitive aspects of the life of any organism: *a* the inner surface, *b* the outer surface, and *c* the sphere of outward behavior. The bodily impulses are represented in the diagram where certain organs connect the outer world with the inner surface of the body, respectively, *1* the oral-facial, *2* anal-urethral, and *3* genital-urethral zones.[1]

In each diagram one impulse is represented as being dominant by means of a heavier line: in I 1 it is the first ("sucking") mode in the oral system. Thus we indicate that we are concerned with that stage of development in which the libido is concentrated mainly in the oral system and serves normally to develop this impulse. Also the circle which represents the surface of the body is more heavily outlined, as is true for all corresponding circles in the diagrams which lie on the diagonal. This indicates that the principle of receptive incorporation legitimately dominates the whole "surface of the body" during the first oral stage. Skin and senses are ready to "drink in" all kinds of perceptual sensations as brought to them by the environment and to enjoy libidinally all kinds of touching, stroking, rocking sensations if they are only kept below the threshold at which motor response would be provoked. The heavy outlining of the outer circle indicates that at this stage social behavior also expresses expectant readiness to receive, as is obvious in the rhythm of waiting, crying, drinking, sleeping. Reactions to stimuli which require more than the holding on with mouth and hands to what has been offered by the environment remain diffuse and uncoördinated. All of this: degree of coördination, muscle and sense development, libido distribution and spontaneous behavior will have to be represented in a final formulation of the first bodily manifestation of our impulse.

II 2

In II 2, the dominating impulse is ⱴ The biting system (gums, jaws, neck, etc.) is in the possession of a relatively high amount of libido and of muscle energy which, at the same time, is manifest throughout the spheres of perception and action; the eyes learn to focus, the ears to locate, the hands

[1] A sixth mode, ⊙ digestive-assimilative "building-up" is vaguely put "inside the body." It will have to be replaced by whatever may in the future best represent the knowledge of the complicated relationships and connections (4, 5, 6) of the inner organs to the social organs, which will prove to be of some importance in regard to connection of body-ego and play structuralization.

to reach out, and the arms to hold. The coördination of
the system necessary for reaching out to an object and the
"plucking" of it for oral incorporation is established. Simultaneously, a change in the concept of the outer world probably occurs. This is represented by the dotted arrow, which
indicates that the incoming object is conceived of in a
somewhat different way than formerly. The object of libidinal interest and of psychobiological training is now the
food. Later it will be faeces and then the genitals. Presumably
each is first conceived of by the infant as belonging inherently
to his own body and subject to his own will, during the first
stages of the development of each zone (I 1, III 3, 4, V 6).
It is only through a sum of psychobiological and cultural
experiences that the child learns that these objects belong to
the environment—an expulsion from the paradise of omnipotence which takes place in the transition from the first (I, III,
V) to the second (II, IV, VI) part of each stage. If we say
psychobiological and cultural influences, we mean for orality
that the changing conditions of the gums and the irresistible
biting impulse, no less than the changing character of the food
and of its delivery, participate in this expulsion into a world
where "in the sweat of thy face thou shalt eat bread till thou
return under the ground".

It is to be regretted that for the sake of orderly procedure
we have to begin with the lower left corner of our chart which
justly should be kept as vague as our knowledge of these stages
of development is dark. But a principle of description to be
used throughout the chart may be explained here: The normal
succession of stages is represented in the diagrams on the diagonal. It is in these stages that impulse and zone find the full
training of their function within the framework of growth and
maturation. A deviation from the normal diagonal development can be horizontal, i.e., progressing to the impulse of the
next stage before the whole organism has integrated the first
stage; or, it can be vertical, i.e., insisting on the impulse of the
first stage when the organism as a whole would be ready for the

training and integration of the dynamic principle of the next stage. Thus, a differentiation of zones and impulses is introduced which gives our chart its two dimensions: in the horizontal we have different impulses connected with one and the same zone—in the vertical we see one and the same impulse connected with different zones.

The stages, as well as their functional characteristics, are, of course, overlapping. The libido, during and after the stages of concentration shown in I 1 and II 2, becomes concentrated in the excretory system, can be pleasurably gratified by the retention and expulsion of the (now more solid) fæces, while, or perhaps just because, the general impulses dominating the rapidly developing sensory and muscular behavior are retaining and expelling. Unlike the previous stages, when incorporation at any cost seemed the rule of behavior, now strong, sometimes "unreasonable", discrimination takes place: sensations are in rapid succession accepted, rejected; objects are clung to stubbornly or thrown away violently; or persons are obstinately demanded or pushed away angrily—tendencies which under the influence of educational factors easily develop into temporary or lasting extremes of self-insistent behavior, maintaining a narcissistic paradise of self-assertive discriminations. The sad truth to be learned in the anal stage and added to the experience of oral phase (which was: "You shall not find pleasure in incorporation except under certain conditions") is: "In your body, your self, your mind, your room, you shall find pleasure in retaining or expelling only under certain conditions."

Thus, the diagonal of the chart indicates and draws up for formulation some normal stages of development, in which certain zones are normally libidinized, certain impulses normally generalized. Where the outer circles are not heavily outlined (in the non-diagonal remainder of the chart) those configurations of impulses can be found which at the particular stage become dominant and generalized only when an abnormal situation arises; though as integrated part tendencies all the impulses are essential for all the zones of a living organism at all times. Wherever a specific case suggests it, the chart might be used to illustrate abnormal correlations by interchanging impulses and by outlining more heavily any untimely generalization of an impulse.

To use the example with which we started: Dr. Sterba's little patient having learned to exchange IV 5, 7 (anal retaining and releasing in accordance with the wishes of the environment) for III 3, 4 (insistence on her own jurisdiction in matters of elimination) managed to keep impulse 3 by partial regression to II 3 and 4 (oral retaining and expelling)—impulses which, of course, are normally developed during the oral phase (closing up against, spitting out of food) but become dominant later only through regression as in this case, or as a result of fixation and retardation—as for example in Case F, where a traumatic combination of constitutional and environmental circumstances had brought about a general "closing up" of body and mind.

In the case of J, we saw the pathological oscillation of the untrained impulses of an eight-year-old boy in the maze of channels which once and for all are established by the experiences of pregenitality: Trained to the toilet without, however, having allowed this training ever to dominate his psychobiological development and to add to his character the traits which are the outcome of having passed through this stage (as would be indicated by IV 5 and IV 6), he used defæcation as a means of expression of an asocial, omnipotent attitude (III 3–III 4). His fantasy of intruding by means of defæcating into an object belonging to an ambivalently loved person would be represented by III 7. When talking about dirty things to the psychiatrist, he expanded impulse 4 over to the oral sphere (II 4) only to refuse all communication (II 3) as soon as the treatment appeared to him to be a punishment. We saw how under treatment the impulse of elimination returned to its original zone and was sublimated. Case K prepared us for a consideration of the phallic phase.

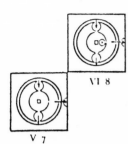

The last two diagrams at the upper end of the diagonal are characterized by the dominance of the tendency to intrude. The general impulse to enter and to do something to another body or to another body's sphere of influence, although existing since earliest orality, is now emphasized and made into a social problem by the rapid development of sense-curiosity and motor-development and the phallic-clitoric erogeneity with its dangerous adherence to incestuous atavisms. Psychobiological emphasis and the forces of education work together at this stage to add another set of sad truths, again leaving it to the child's ego organization to make the best of it: "Not only the inner and outer surface of one's body and the zones connecting inside and outside are under foreign jurisdiction, but also those forces and organs which single out and seek fascinating objects in the environment in an ecstasy of action." "You may have the pleasure of touching and entering and finding out only under certain conditions."

Girls, as we know, have a shorter or longer period of phallic tendencies (with clitoral erogeneity and the fantasy of having or achieving a penis) corresponding to the general development of the intrusive impulse. The question of when and in what way this phase is passed through and overcome, has aroused much controversy in psychoanalysis. Here, too, direct observation of play might prove a *via regia*. It seems certain that the penis-wish is absorbed more or less completely by the wish for a baby. The girl, following her destiny, which is to libidinize, develop and train a second organ system of incorporation with her procreative organs as its center, can be said to undergo a partial regression to the generalized sensitivity and receptive behavior first manifested during the oral stages. Thus in the last line of the chart we tentatively characterize female destiny by adding a procreative-protective impulse to the impulse of self-preservation "inside the body". Whenever the chart is used for a female subject or patient, this impulse should be outlined more heavily and generalized in order to give zones and impulses, as well as the surface of the body and the motor sphere, a new specifically female-procreative correlation.[1] It is this correlation which differentiates the female tendency to incorporate from sexual passivity in men.

The integration of all the vital impulses is essential and indispensable to physical, psychic and mental self-preservation and for social and sexual intercourse. Whatever one does, it is essential that one be able to accept, to keep, to digest and to eliminate; to give and to receive; to take and to be taken in fair ratio. We find that the under- or over-development of one impulse decisively changes the organization of all the others and creates a more or less pathological "type of personality". There are "suckers", "biters", "retainers", "expellers", and "intruders" in all fields of human life. One could say that without them there would not be so many various "fields" in life. And there are types of personality which suffer from impotence in one or more of these impulses. As the Arapesh says: "There are those whose ears are open and whose throats are open; those whose ears are open and whose throats are shut; those whose ears are shut and whose throats are open; and those whose ears and throats are both shut".[2]

The schematization of which we have been guilty might find an excuse in the fact that its aim is not only to help organize very simple infantile acts, but also the most primitive concepts the child has of his own organism, and the theories and expec-

[1] A later, mature level of this correlation, characterologically and pathologically not independent from this first pregenital level, may be seen in the circle of conception (more or less active incorporation) pregnancy and parturition (more or less retentive or eliminative) and lactation (in which the woman accomplishes more or less the long desired equivalent of intrusive generosity). Men find a fulfilment of this correlation in the sublimation of creative work.

[2] Mead, Margaret: *Sex and Temperament*. New York: William Morrow & Co., 1935, p. 27.

tations he develops in projecting his concepts onto others. Here, as we know, the origin of some typical dreams and fears may be found, such as being swallowed or robbed (by "suckers" and "biters"), being jailed and bound (by "retainers"), driven away and banished (by "expellers"), stabbed and raped (by "intruders").

This, then, is the system of zones and impulses which form the organic basis for the normal or irregular appearance of configurations such as those described in connection with G's, J's and K's autocosmic, microcosmic and macrocosmic behavior. The impulses are developed and, as it were, trained at their zones of origin during the (overlapping) stages of child development characterized by the general tendency to *incorporation* (oral-respiratory, nutritional, sensory-tactual), retentive-eliminative *discrimination* (muscular, anal-urethral), and *intrusion* (motor, phallic-urethral). In the course of phylogenetic and ontogenetic development the organ-modes are estranged (because overdue or precocious) from their original zones and can be observed as seeking new manifestations: the organism offers a limited range of safe displacements in habits and minor symptoms; reality allows for certain systems of projections; society accepts the expression through action of a number of character traits. The world of play affords opportunity to experiment with organ-modes in extrabodily arrangements which are physiologically safe, socially permissible, physically workable and psychologically satisfying.

IV.

PLAY CONSTRUCTIONS OF COLLEGE STUDENTS*

Interest in the psychology of play ranges from the first playful movements of the baby to the various manifestations of the need for play in adults. Taking the most fascinating extremes of "play", that of the child on the one hand and the productions of the artist on the other, we find that in spite of the·

* Report on a procedure conducted as a part of the Studies in Personality at the Harvard Psychological Clinic (Dr. Henry A. Murray).

testimony of language popular opinion tends to evaluate them as antithetical phenomena, finding no "sense" in children's play, while looking at the artist's play as a phenomenon burdened—and in modern times, overburdened—with conscious problems and meanings.

When the writer undertook to participate in the studies of the Harvard Psychological Clinic on the development and character-formation of a group of average young college men his interest in the psychology of play led him to place these subjects in a play situation in order to observe what their late adolescent imaginations would do with it.

Description of the Procedure

Each subject was brought into a room in which there was a table covered with small toys. He was told that the observer (who was unknown to him) was interested in ideas for movie plays, and wished him to use these toys to construct on a second table a *dramatic scene*. After answering a few typical questions (e.g., "Do I have to use all the toys?"), the observer left the room for fifteen minutes, but watched the behavior of the subject through a one-way mirror. In the following pages these first observations, made while the subject believed that he was unobserved, are referred to as the *Preparatory Period*. After fifteen minutes the observer reëntered the room, wrote down the subject's explanations and sketched the scene (referred to as the *Dramatic Scene*).

Some of the toys were provided in large numbers, e.g., farmers, animals, furniture, automobiles, and blocks. To most of the subjects the principal toys suggested a family, consisting of father, mother, son, daughter, and a little girl. In addition, there was a maid and a policeman. It may be added that these toys were chosen without deliberate purpose according to what was available at the nearest toy store.

Results

Five out of 22 subjects ignored the instructions and on the observer's return greeted him in a friendly way with some such remark as, "Everything quiet! Just a nice, harmonious, country scene!" Of the remaining seventeen subjects, only 4 constructed dramatic scenes which were not automobile accidents, while 13 subjects put in the center either an automobile accident or an arrangement which prevented one. Nine times in these scenes the little girl was the object of danger or the victim of an accident, other female toys twice. In other parts of these same scenes 7 female toys died, fainted, were kidnapped or were bitten by a dog. In all, 18 female toys (the little girl 10 times) and no male figures were in danger or perished, a theme which can be called the typical fantasy of the average member of the group. On the other hand, in the construction of the subject who could be classified as the most masculine and socially best adapted member, a dog was the victim of an accident. The red racer with its not specifically named driver came to grief in the constructions of the two subjects who respectively came nearest to manifest homosexuality and to manifest psychosis.

Interpretation of Results

The examples to be given in this report will illustrate a few hypotheses which follow from the analysis of the results.

They suggest first that the five friendly subjects had not failed to understand the instructions but that they could not construct a dramatic scene, because they had to suppress their first (most probably unconscious) response which corresponded to some traumatic childhood event (or to a screen memory which embraced a number of traumatic childhood experiences).

On the other hand, in most of those scenes which dared to be dramatic, traumatic childhood memories appeared either in the Preparation Time or in the Dramatic Scene—in the form of some characteristic symbolic fantasy, usually of an accident in which the little girl, rarely one of the other female figures, was the victim.

The constructed scenes will, of course, be the central object of our analytic efforts. We use as associative material whatever the subject said or did just before or just after the construction of his scene, which seemed to be related in content or form specifically to what he did or said in other interviews and experiments.[1] This specificity was taken as the basis for interpretation only after it had been established in conference with other observers.[2]

I.

M: Zeeno

1. *Preparatory Period.* The first toy that Zeeno touched was one of the twin beds. He set it at the extreme edge of

[1] The experimental or interview procedures of the Harvard Psychological Clinic mentioned in this report are:

1. *Conference.* (Dr. Henry A. Murray) The first session for the subject was the Conference. The subject sat down at a table with the 5 members of the Diagnostic Council. He was asked questions and given certain tests to perform in their presence.

2. *Autobiography.* (Dr. Henry A. Murray) The subject was asked to write for 2 hours about his early life and development. He was presented with an outline to guide him.

3. *Childhood Memories.* (H. Scudder Mekeel) The subject was given a questionnaire pertaining to family relations, and he was interviewed twice (each session one hour) and asked to give as many memories as possible of his childhood and adolescence.

4. *Sexual Development.* (Dr. William G. Barrett) The subject was asked to lie on a couch and say what came to his mind. Later, he was asked various questions about his sexual development.

5. *Hypnotic Test.* (Robert W. White) In two sessions, an attempt was made to hypnotize the subjects and a numerical score assigned representing his susceptibility to hypnosis. On a later day, a different interviewer encouraged him to discuss the test at length.

6. *Thematic Apperception Test.* (Christiana D. Morgan) The subject was shown a series of dramatic pictures. He was asked to make up a story for which each picture might be used as an illustration.

7. *Imaginal Productivity Test.* (David R. Wheeler) (a) Beta Ink Blot test. The subject was asked to tell what forms he could make out in the ink blots. (b) Similes test. The subject was asked to make up similes for certain words (presented to him in succession by the E). (c) Minister's Black Veil test. The subject was asked to spend an hour writing a story using as a theme the appearance of a minister in the pulpit with a black veil over his eyes. (Hawthorne).

[2] Unfortunately such a partial report as this one cannot convincingly demonstrate this specificity. The sceptical reader is referred to the Clinic's forthcoming publication which, in addition to further reports of procedures with the same subjects, contains detailed biographical studies. (The names used in this report are those used in the Clinic's material.)

the table beyond the edge of the sheet of paper. He did the same with the other twin bed on the opposite edge so that they were *as far away as possible from each other*. (Figure 10.) Next he placed a wall which separated a couch from the beds. Then the bathroom was constructed and separated; the kitchen followed but was given no wall; neither had the house as such any surrounding walls.

Next he took, as the first toy person, the maid. Here, Zeeno was doubtful for a time—put the toy back and in a nervous

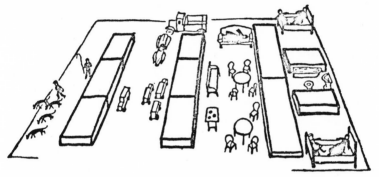

FIGURE 10

manner touched the region of his penis. He looked around the room with a worried expression, then shifted to a street scene. First he placed the cars (the red racer and the green truck) and then outlined the street (just as in the house scene he had first placed the furniture and then built the walls of the rooms). Now he seemed able suddenly to continue more rapidly, obviously lost in that concentration characteristic of undisturbed play. He placed other cars in more rapid succession, then put people quickly and decisively at certain places, keeping males separate from females, and the daughter from the rest of the family.

2. *The Dramatic Scene.* When the observer entered the room, Zeeno exclaimed, "There is not enough space in this house", and added quickly and anxiously, as if he did not believe himself, "Shall I tell you why the son and the father sleep in one bed? Because the mother, of course, has to be near

the kitchen, and the daughter sleeps in the dining room because the maid has to be near the kitchen, too. The green truck drives on the highway and the red racer has to stop suddenly. Here (pointing to the extreme left of the scene) is a fisherman. He is disturbed by a man with his four dogs who is looking for a lost lamb."

3. The manifest content of this use of the play material raises several analytic questions: Where is the dramatic scene which the subject was asked to construct? In the house everybody is asleep. Furthermore only those walls are built which separate people—not the outer walls which make a house and a home. The need to keep things separate is paramount: bed, wall, couch, wall; men, women, their positions only weakly rationalized. In the street a collision is prevented—a dubious dramatic element. Likewise the scene at the left at most only implies a drama, i.e., a lamb has been lost—an accident in the past, not a dramatic scene in the present. What is it that has to be separated and why? What do the subject's childhood memories suggest in regard to these ideas?

The biography calls our attention to the following event: "Zeeno used to sleep in the same room with a sister who died. . . . She died about three o'clock in the morning before the doctor arrived." He remembers "lying in bed not particularly concerned about this". Nevertheless the examiner to whom the subject tells this story reports that: "He has a little anxiety about this. He was silent for some time afterwards."

From dream interpretations we know that the dream often disguises the sleeper's deep inner participation in a scene by having him see himself as a "not particularly concerned" on-looker. The psychoanalyst of children can add to this well-confirmed interpretation the actual experience of having seen children accept a traumatic experience, especially the death of a relative, with complete calm, although every detail of a later neurosis may indicate the pathogenic importance of this same event. It is possible that a feeling of guilt may torment Zeeno in connection with this death, about which he denies any natural anxiety. Children who mourn in this "invisible" way are often deeply concerned with the idea that some aggressive or sexual act or wish of their own might have been the cause of the death of the ambivalently loved person.

Several times during the various interviews Zeeno voiced thoughts of death. When, in the conference, he was asked of what he was most afraid, Zeeno answered, "That I am not going to live terribly long." To one of the ink blots he said, "I immediately think of a skeleton and ribs, and on each side above I see two faces looking at each other, guarding these ribs with an austere expression, like twins"—a detail which may be significant in considering the rôle which certain twins played in his life as can be read in his biography. He had shared the bedroom with his second sister after the first had died. At the very time of his sister's illness Zeeno remembers having had "mimic intercourse" with an older girl several times, either one of his sisters, or more probably one of their friends. Experiences with girls, however, and punishments connected with them, seem to have come into associative connection with his sister's death. It may have been some such anxiety which he was trying to overcome by the repeated self-assurance: "I know a lot of people older than myself who have actually asked me to advise them on certain (sexual) subjects. This always made me think that my advice was pretty good."

When he talked about his actual sexual experiences, Zeeno's language became especially queer and detached: "I never mingle in intimate relations." . . . "I have never desired to indulge with a virgin." . . . "I decided I might indulge in sexual congress." . . . "Having found a suitable person, I took part in coitus on various occasions." In such carefully chosen expressions we see an effort to separate the experience from its affect, a tendency which is obvious both in Zeeno's thinking and living—and in the formal elements of his play construction.

As for the search for the lost lamb, the part of the scene, which in spite of its inconspicuous position at the edge of the table, approached a dramatic content more nearly than any other part: I assume that it represented the unanswered question in the subject's mind, as to "what happened to the lamb",

the little sister. Other details of this scene which could confirm
our interpretation reveal more about the actual family constellation of the subject's childhood than is permissible to
quote.

4. *General remarks.* In selecting and comparing certain
elements of the subject's memories and of his play, we point to
the *probable* importance of a certain event in his life. As a
psychic reality, we assume, the theme of that traumatic event
still imposes both its content, and certain structural elements
as well, on the subject's autoplastic and alloplastic behavior,
i.e., it imposes certain configurations upon an arrangement of
toys on a table.[1] In Zeeno's case we suggest the interpretation
that in his life as well as in his play construction he has to separate certain elements because their connection arouses anxiety
in him, and that these elements correspond to the details of
his experiences with his sister. In this short account we are
forced to neglect the fact that in the formulation of every
psychic theme it is possible to interchange active and passive,
subject and object, without having the theme lose either its
importance or its inner truth; that is to say, we may assume
that Zeeno is afraid to die young (like his sister) according to
the primitive notion of "an eye for an eye", or that he, the
younger, felt himself to have been seduced by his sister, or
shared some kind of guilt with her and was afraid of having to
die as she did.

Other interpretations may suggest themselves to the careful
reader of the subject's biography. Our conclusion is that he
was unable to construct a dramatic situation but revealed only
at the very edge the traumatic situation in his memory which
struggled for expression when, at our authoritative suggestion
"to play", a safety valve was opened and quickly closed again.

N: Berry

1. *Preparatory Period.* Without any hesitation Berry builds
the form shown in Figure 11a. Then he changes the form and
constructs a scene (playing with, contemplating, and at first

[1] In Kurt Lewin's terms: A "structuralization of the life-space" represented
in play, a material which is less "refractory" than actual life.

rejecting the maid as did more than half of the group): The father and mother discover the son with the maid in the kitchen (Figure 11b). But he does not like this scene. He builds another house, without doors, in which the kitchen is

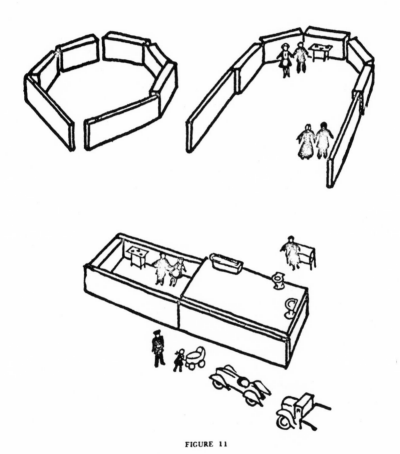

FIGURE 11

separated from the living room and the son and maid from the parents, who, in addition, are completely shut in by a ceiling— the only one to be found in these constructions.

2. *The Dramatic Scene.* (Figure 11c) He explains the scene more impersonally than the other subjects do. "The owner of

the house and his wife, a visitor in the kitchen." Behind the house in the garden sits "a member of the family", and on the street the policeman stops traffic in order to let the little girl pass safely.

3. *Comments.* Again where we vainly awaited a dramatic situation, we find only the indirect suggestion of drama which is implicit in the effort to avoid discovery and accident.

Among the subject s memories occurs the following scene: At the age of six—a garden behind the house, a little girl with whom he eats onions. He kisses the girl. One day the girl doesn't come back. She is not allowed to come any more. "Is this because of me?" he asks his mother. "I doubt it", is the answer. In this moment he says he learned what it meant to doubt—a statement which justifies our taking this scene seriously. An event recurring in his later childhood awoke in him this bitter feeling of doubt again and again, doubt of the justice of his parents. If he had a quarrel with his sister, the parents usually intervened in her favor.

Discovery, intervention, punishment appear in a rather decisive way in the material of the Clinic: For example, the subject relates that Hawthorne's vicar wears the black veil because he had discovered his brother with a woman. The vicar thus in wearing the veil punishes himself for what he has seen. In the autobiography we find the statement: "I had an exceptionally curious mind regarding sex matters and read a great variety of medical books from the age of ten to fifteen." This may throw light on a neurotic difficulty in reading. This inhibition however had a prior history, Berry having developed first an inhibition against play with girls or touching them at all, especially his sister. Later this inhibition extended to reading, in which his curiosity obviously had found refuge. Visions of the past, so he says, came between him and the reading matter; and it tormented him that there should be so little personal feeling in these visions—a subjective account of that separation of experience and affect which we found in Zeeno.

His first house-form (Figure 11a) suggests a diagrammatic cross-section of a female pelvis. Here he himself has formed that which he perceives in the ink blot test: "Cross-section through a female body, as one sees it in medical books." Other blots remind him of embryos or portions of a miscarriage; others of ulcers and decomposed animals. Thus the house seems first to represent the (female) body, which contains what he wants to know. It then takes the form of a real house which contains the body which one wants to know about: hence, man, maid, and intervention. But Berry remembers that if one tries to enter and discover the secret, one is discovered oneself and separated from the object of one's curiosity. Therefore, it seems better to avoid discovery by separating all dangerous elements right at the beginning. Thus, in his play construction, parents are enclosed so that they are unable to discover the son (nor can he, we may add, see what they are doing). This avoidance again (as in Zeeno's case) has its parallel in a precaution on the street: the traffic is stopped in order to let the little girl pass safely. In this way a traumatic outcome is avoided, but at the same time a dramatic situation has become impossible.

Separated and alone, " a member of the family" sits behind the house in the special arrangement similar to Zeeno's "sister". She may well be the girl in the garden behind the house of his childhood, the girl whose disappearance caused or was caused by guilt. Certainly it must be significant that through all of these constructions wherever we are able to sense the persistence of concern for a person who disappeared during childhood, this person is represented by a toy which is placed outside of a closed house or room and always to the right of the subject. In one case, the "best boy" of the group, a dead rival-cousin, was even placed on another table where he "walked in safety". One cannot help comparing this with the custom of some primitive peoples who make a hole in their houses through which they push the corpses of their dead, only to close it again so that the dead cannot come back into the house. Neither Zeeno's nor Berry's house had doors and we find a house without doors in the constructions of the subjects in whose mind the idea of death and sex are closely linked: the

dark room whence we come (the womb, the inside of the female
body) and the one where we go (the tomb, the beyond).
Symbolically these are one idea in primitive thought and may
become permanently associated by a traumatic experience
occurring at that age and stage of childhood for which this
association, in an abortive form, is typical (the phallic-sadistic
stage of libido-organization).

Here we might make another suggestion. So far as the first
house-form represented a cross-section through a female body
it contained a secret with which Berry was much concerned, as
is suggested by his history as well as his ink blot fantasies of
embryos and miscarriages. In his childhood he had heard that
before he was born his mother had given birth to a girl who
died—a fact which had strengthened his sexual and medical
curiosity and influenced his mental development.

O: Asper

Because of its extreme emphasis on separation a construction
which showed the most psychotic elements is of special clinical
interest.

1 and 2. *Preparatory Period and Dramatic Scene.* (Figure
12) Asper places six peasants near one another like soldiers.
Then he stares at them for several minutes, looking very un-
happy, almost as if paralyzed. Thereupon he arranges some
cars: In the green truck he puts a policeman; smaller cars and a
man are approaching with a dog. Again follows a long, paralyzed hesitation, as if a single movement would bring about a
catastrophe. Suddenly he crashes the red racer into a block so
that it overturns. Immediately after this the subject seems freer,
as if a magic word had been spoken, and completes the scene
quickly. He puts the little girl into a corner and surrounds
her by animals. He surrounds the policeman's car with
peasants and turns the peasant with the dog so that he "leaves
the field" (as Kurt Lewin would put it).

3. *Comments.* When the observer enters the room the subject says, "The imagination does not have enough to work on.

Everything here is symbolical." About the little girl he adds: "She does not understand what it is all about. The animals are her pets." About the green truck: "An army truck. These men could easily be taken into the truck." (He puts them in.) . . . About the peasant: "He is immune to all of us, he lives in the woods, he is outside, he can't be touched."

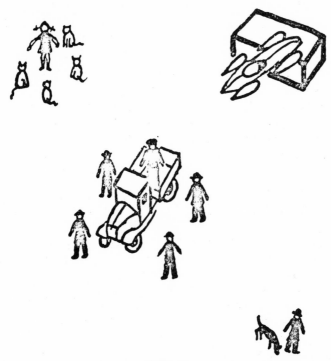

FIGURE 12

The subject in his nearness to mental disintegration (elsewhere he says that even the word " 'incongruous' becomes meaningless after a while") was the only subject who felt that his play construction was symbolic; while at the same time, paradoxically but significantly enough, he was the one who of the whole group felt most keenly that the dangers of playing were real. Nearer to "catastrophe" than any of the other subjects, he scarcely dared to move. He maintained a careful organization of cars and soldiers, gradually placed the soldiers closer and closer to the policeman, and felt easier only after he had rendered the red racer innocuous. The peasant with his dog goes silently away: "He is outside, he can't be touched."

Much could be said about the psychotic characteristics of this play construction:[1] how the danger of symbolic expression in infantile material is feared as if it were a real danger, how the plot shrinks to a mere spatial arrangement whose function it is to make everything, "right in time, right in space, not too late, not too soon, just right", as one of the inmates of the Worcester State Hospital remarked when he showed me his construction.

It is because of this need to maintain psychic barriers to protect themselves from infantile chaos, that out of 40 normal, neurotic and psychotic adults and children the only person to protest against the test as "childish", was an inmate of the Worcester State Hospital. He had said that he could build an accident, but refrained from it. Instead, he merely placed the furniture, people, cars and animals in curved rows. At one point he started to put the little girl into a bed, but smiled thoughtfully and gave it up to arrange another long row of toys. Reminded by the observer that he wanted to build an accident, he said: "Well, well, well, a child might do that, if it cared to." Then for a moment he threw the cars around furiously, as if illustrating what a child would do. Thereupon he began setting the blocks two and two together, and said, "Some people forget their childhood, others go back to it." Then, as he built a solid square of block he said, "This could be the foundation for a house—or wharf. And this", putting two blocks together, "is a breakwater. It is supposed to turn waves backwards." After a thoughtful moment he began to whirl the breakwater around as if it were helpless against the waves, and said slowly, "Do you think—a wave—can flow—backwards?"

[1] See also Rosenzweig, Saul, and Shakow, David: *Play Technique in Schizophrenia and Other Psychoses, II. An Experimental Study of Schizophrenic Constructions with Play Materials.* Amer. J. of Orthopsychiat., VII, 1937. p. 36.

II

"Let nothing happen to the girls and let nothing happen anyway", seemed to be the slogan of the small group of cautious subjects represented by Zeeno and Berry, who by the separation of dangerous play elements demonstrated to us the compulsive character's technique of prevention. "Let something happen but let it happen to the girl" is the slogan of the majority, whose spokesman we shall describe next.

P: Oriol

1. *Preparatory Period.* After receiving his instructions the subject jokes. He takes the toy toilet between his fingers and smiles broadly at the observer. Left to himself he grows serious: Let's see. Little girl? No. Maid? No. Baby carriage? No. (Highly dissatisfied.) Suddenly, with sweeping movements, he makes three piles—people, cars, blocks. He then finds excited satisfaction in taking single objects out of the piles and constructing his scene.

In the center of his construction he first puts a policeman standing on a block with four cars pointing straight at him from four directions. If real, this scene could represent only a suicidal demonstration against the authority of the state. And, although in the final scene he had turned the cars so that they were not pointing at the policeman, his first remark when the observer entered the room continued the theme of revolt.

2. *The Dramatic Scene.* (Figure 13) "This is like the Place de la Concorde, where the riots were." Of the policeman, "He stands in his box higher than the other people" (suggesting probably something like the Napoleon column in the Place Vendôme). The little girl is run over—thus suffering the fate for which at first the policeman was destined—"because the maid chats with an old friend of her mother and does not watch the girl". The parents, by coincidence, arrive at this moment and are witnesses to their daughter's death.

On leaving, the subject again takes the toilet, laughs and says, "I suppose some people use this to express their ideas. I haven't come to that stage."

3. *Comments:* Though the subject jokes twice about the toy toilet, he assures us, without being asked, that he does not use this medium through which he supposes "some people" express their ideas. This, and his strange pleasure in piling the toys and in taking single pieces out of the piles, arouses a suspicion as to the psychic reality of a painful element in the subject's memories. At the age of eight (an unusually advanced age for the breaking through of aggression in this direction) Oriol was

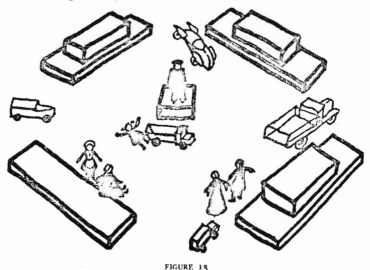

FIGURE 13

found *smearing fæces.* This story is often repeated at home to family intimates, much to his discomfort, and is advanced by his family as a reason for wondering how he ever got into college.

In addition to the riot topic and the hints regarding the *anal riot* of his childhood, there are in his construction spatial arrangements which indicate what may be the main psychic and physiological quandary of his life, i.e., to retain or release. First he builds one street, then a square with four entrances, and finally points out explicitly that the square has many exits. We may add that no one who had heard the subject talk would fail to remark his speech, which often approaches an *oral riot—*

a flow of intellectually defiant words which he releases continuously. He is said to have learned to talk very late.

Oriol likes to play with the idea of running away from home;
but he has decided to run away only intellectually. He keeps
silent when with his father, but remains intellectually his own
boss, and says so to whoever wants or does not want to listen.
While his memories are full of humiliating experiences, his
confessions express the wish to overcome humiliation through
greatness, and to overcome unclean tendencies by producing
beauty. "If I could remodel the world I would like to be the
greatest writer." But, "I am afraid of life and afraid of death."
Sure to be humiliated whenever he expresses his immature and
unconsolidated impulses, he must choose masochistic wish ful-
filments in order to gain satisfaction. He wants to be a poet—
but he wants to be a martyr poet. "I want to expose myself
and suffer." Here, even were it not suggested by other constructions as well, one would suspect that the girl in the accident represents the subject himself whose parents thus witness
his suffering.

Of his construction, Oriol is right in saying, "I haven't come
to the stage where I would use the toilet to express my ideas",
for he obviously prefers a suicidal accident to a riot, after the
fæcal riot of his past (playing with fæces) is suggested to him
by the stimulus situation of being asked to play. But in
spite of his objection, he must repeat the event he wants
to avoid in the formal elements of his construction (piling:
playing).

4. *Second Construction.* A year later Oriol was asked to
construct another dramatic scene. In evaluating such a repetition we must remember that the earlier construction had taken
20 minutes, had not been understood by the subject as "meaning" anything, and had not been mentioned to him by anybody
afterwards. Again Oriol piles the blocks before he starts. This
time his square is first round with one exit leading to the water.
A truck coming from the direction of the water is headed
straight for the policeman. There is a dog in front of the
truck. "It will not be run over" the rebellious subject says, a

fact which we shall recall later when, in reviewing the construction of the well-educated and pious Mauve, a dog is run over. In changing the square, all form is abandoned, the blocks and furniture appear in piles. Again the memorial for a revolutionist takes the center and this time it is a communist worker. Quite independent of this scene, another part of the table is supposed to be the inside of a house. Here a little girl stands in front of a mirror "admiring herself and stubborn". "She is defiant. She does not like people. Later, she will go to the maid who cannot tell her to 'shut up!' " This parallel to the communistic orator on the memorial characterizes well the state of continuous, narcissistic, and oral revolt in which our subject lives.

When the observer reënters the room, Oriol has the red racer in his hand. After having given his other explanations, he adds it to the scene, remarking as if excusing himself, "This one does not mean anything." Then, in going out, he says: "I left the bathroom empty. I would be embarrassed—". Thus, he seems to follow the pattern of his first construction which he had left with the words, "I suppose some people use this (the toilet) to express their ideas. I haven't come to that stage." We have seen how far this last negation really was a double affirmation; we may assume the same about the protested unimportance of the red racer.

5. *Remarks.* Oriol's construction shows the confusion which can extend to the adolescent mind from childhood experiences in an almost tragi-comic way. Only with weak negations does he separate himself from the most embarrassing childhood situations. A need to expose himself must have been decisive in this construction.

Oriol did not talk when he was expected to; he still soiled when he was no longer expected to do so—and this "stubbornness" (which might well be based on a constitutional or early traumatic factor) still prevades everything he says and does with typical pregenital ambivalence. Not independent enough to do without love and protection, he still is not able to return

love because this would have meant in childhood the uncondi-
tional surrender of the jurisdiction over parts of his body and
now would mean the final socialization of modes of behavior
which are derived from those organic functions. Oriol does
not soil, because he is neither child nor psychotic; nevertheless,
elimination and retention in their characterological and mental
aspects are his problem. What is presented here by Oriol in
his chaotic way in regard to anal-sadistic characteristics, differs
only quantitatively, not qualitatively, from the general problems facing our whole group of late adolescents. Did their
genitality make itself independent of regressive association with
the psychobiologically significant drives of childhood? We
know that the absence of genital consolidation necessitates a
continuous state of defense against the guerilla warfare of
infantile impulses which still resist "don'ts" which have long
since become senseless, infantile impulses, which promise non-
existent paradises, and which urge the individual to subdue
love objects or to surrender to them—in an oscillation between
love and hate.

Since we may be criticized for the clinical predilections in
our observation of a group of individuals who did not come as
patients, it might be of special interest to compare with the
illustration of Oriol's fixation on oral and anal-sadistic autoerotism, the construction of Mauve, who was perhaps the best
organized personality in the group. His construction shows a
typical attempt to overcome the pregenital ambivalence menac-
ing the best organized young men in their relationships with
the other sex. Between Oriol and Mauve lies the problem of
the whole group: how, in a society, which with moral and economic means discourages unbroken psychosexual progress, can
one adapt without sacrificing one's genital masculinity; how
develop without rebellion; how wait without regression; how
love without suspicion, fear and hate; in a word, how overcome ambivalence, the counterpart of obedience? This is the
moral problem of adolescence which various cultures deal with
in various ways.

Q: Mauve

1. *Preparatory Period.* Mauve took off his coat and, obviously pleased with himself and ready to serve scientific purposes, began his construction like a good organizer, quickly and without interruption. A growing excitement was evident—he got caught by his ideas.

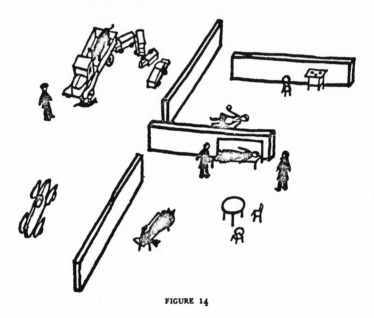

FIGURE 14

2. *The Dramatic Scene.* (Figure 14) Mauve explains: "The green truck is running over a dog—it is the little girl's dog." A car coming after it bumps into the truck, a second one is just turning over, a third one tries to avoid the crash. In the kitchen "the maid is fainting; she has a little dog herself and this is the reason why she feels like that." In the living room we see "a young lady on the couch in the first stage of pneumonia. Something very emotional in this scene. Her fiance and her doctor are looking down on her. The mother does not feel well and has gone to bed."

3. *Comments:* This is the only time a dog is run over instead

of a woman; we are therefore interested to hear Mauve in another interview say: "Women are faithful, they are dogs. They have been dogs for so many centuries." In his outlook on life, as well as in his conception of himself, we see him separate himself from the "animal in us". "My standards are high and I intend to keep them." Woman and drives belong to another, an animalistic world which is separated from the young man's world of clear standards.

On the other hand, standards are derived from his education by his mother and other women. Many years younger than the father, the mother is deeply attached to the son and he accounts for their emotional relationship in the most explicit œdipus fantasy offered by any of the group.[1] Over-obedient to her wishes, he says, he "almost dedicated his life to the avoidance of drinking, smoking and swearing". And yet certain circumstances in his relationship to his mother seem to draw him deeply into ambivalence towards the weaker sex.

His mother is "handicapped by a disease which periodically disables her completely" and she always tried to keep the healthy, active boy close to home, of which he complains, though taking care of his mother in a most touching manner. If, in the "dog running on the street" we want to see a symbolic rebellion of the son against all the careful obedience which a physically weakened authority is imposing on him, we may understand that it is his drive, the "animal in us", which is punished by being run over. On the other hand—the dog represents the group of human beings to whom something happens: i.e., women.

If we confront this subject's outbreak with his remarks about women on the one side and his educational indebtedness to his, mother and other women on the other, a conscious or unconscious duality of attitude towards women, quite common in our civilization, is represented: men easily identify women with the wishes which they stimulate. If they learn to have contempt for "lower" drives (and their pregenital components) they may also have contempt for women so far as they are the

[1] See the Clinic's publication.

objects of their wishes. As beings, however, held in high esteem ("mother, aunt, teacher") women are also identified with the strictest and most idealistic concepts of conscience. "Angels" or "dogs"—women awaken uncomfortable ambivalent feelings, feelings which spoil the perspective of sex life. A not unusual type of rather well adapted young men (whom Mauve seems to represent) learns to live and to care for a world of achievements which have "nothing to do with women"; it is characteristic of this type that in order to satisfy his conscious and potent genital wishes he goes "to Paris"—as Mauve says he plans to do. There, then, women are neither angels nor dogs; they are French. The girl who does not belong to one's own culture or class (in other constructions often the girl who does not belong to the family, namely, the maid) is the object of more conscious fantasies.

4. *General remarks.* We may ask however what the little girl, to whom the subjects pay so much damaging attention, might represent. It is hard to give the reader an impression of the uncanny regularity with which these young men whether normal, neurotic or psychotic examined the little girl and, as if they were following a ritualistic duty, seriously put her under the green or red car, or placed a policeman in the center of the scene to protect her. The majority of the subjects who failed to have this theme in their final scene at least considered it and rehearsed it during the preparatory period. A great number of problems must be evoked by this little girl and the crux of the problem must be symbolized by the accidents which happen to her.

Some of the possible explanations, all suggested by material which cannot be quoted here in full are:

a.) The little girl may represent a little girl of importance (i.e., a sister) in the subject's childhood. The uniform and typical handling of this toy suggests, however, that she represents rather a symbol than an historical individual.

b.) The little girl, as the youngest among the toys, might appear to be the representative of "the child", the most endangered and therefore the most protected human being in traffic.

Can we assume that in spite of the abundance of dramatic moments in life and literature, movies and newspapers, accidents resulting in the death of children are emotionally important enough to be the dramatic scene par excellence for the majority of twenty Harvard students? In that case, our psychoanalytic explanations are less valuable, though not entirely worthless since they show the unconscious meaning of this accident in its relationship to other unconscious concepts of "what happens to children".

c.) The emphasis may lie on *girl*. Since, according to common infantile theories, girls are made into girls, not born as such, some violence is assumed to exist in sexual matters. The accident, then, which belongs to the "complex" of related symbols dominating our construction, may represent the act of violence of which girls are the victims.

d.) Since, beside the little girl, the victims in these accidents are always and only female toys, the little girl may represent a *pars pro toto*, namely, the female world, in which case it might have been selected because it provokes the least conscious aggressive fantasies and allows the subject to feel himself consciously free of any participation in the committed violence. We shall presently come back to this point.

e.) The little girl may represent a *totum pro parte*. Freud, in the Interpretation of Dreams (p. 338), remarks that in dreams "children often signify the genitals since men and women are in the habit of referring to their *genital organs* as 'little man', 'little woman', 'little thing'. To play with or to beat a little child is often the dream's representation of *masturbation*." It is a big step from our first tentative explanation to this interpretation; but the reader will have to decide to make this step with us tentatively—or to leave the question open. Psychoanalytic method, waiting for the most part for associative material in order to interpret any product of the mind, uses only a few "established" symbols, uniform "translation" of which has proved to be necessary and suitable in long and exhaustive studies.

Two of these symbols with which we are concerned here are

put together by Freud in a title to the interpretation of a woman's dream which states bluntly: "The 'little one' as the genital organ. Being run over as a symbol of sexual intercourse." (*Op. cit.*, p. 342.) Dream interpretation thus suggests that what the subjects do with the little girl corresponds in their unconscious with ideas of autoerotic and alloerotic sexual acts, in which something happens to the partner's or the subject's own sexual organs. There is nothing in their strange behavior which a priori could devaluate such a strange notion.

f.) We cannot avoid pointing to a sociological factor, namely, the sexual life typical for such a group of biologically mature individuals as our subjects. Their sexual activities are autoerotic, or else consist of a kind of mutual (heterosexual) autoerotism, more or less sanctioned by society. The danger of this form of gratification is the conditioning of masculine impulses by the repetition of a situation with infantile characteristics. Whenever the mature drive is aroused, *the impulse of masculine intrusion* and certain related sadistic tendencies are mobilized with all the other impulses which participate in the pattern of complete sexual satisfaction. In mere sex play they fail to be satisfied and—as it were—to be disarmed. It is, I think, this frustrated intrusive component of masculinity, which, though continuously stimulated in our subjects, has not yet found its wholesome amalgamation with the other factors of heterosexual partnership, and which therefore in their secret fantasies appears in a certain *homicidal and suicidal* rudeness—which, we may add here, has an important sociological counterpart in certain adolescent and cruel forms of public sensationalism not dissimilar in content to our constructions.

g.) Female subjects who constructed scenes with the same toys showed as a common factor the criminal man (father). The five college girls among them (the same age as our subjects) constructed the following scenes:

R: A father who was a deserter in war and lives in shameful exile, picks up on the street a little girl who has been run over by a truck. She is his daughter.

S: A selfish father, who had neglected his wife and children for years, comes home and finds everything destroyed and. everybody killed by a flood.

T: A father, supposedly away in an insane asylum, comes home to murder his family.

U: A landowner strangles his wife. His servant's daughter, to whom he had made advances, testifies against him at the trial.

V: Robbers steal a table out of a house in the middle of the night.

It would be interesting if further studies would substantiate that to the main theme of our male subjects ("Something happens or is prevented from happening to a girl"), there corresponds a female one: "A man is (or is prevented from being) criminally aggressive." The fact that—with a few exceptions—both sexes place a member of the opposite sex in the center of the construction, points clearly to a sexual component in scenes which on the conscious level refer to danger and death.

W: Krumb

1. *Preparatory Period and Dramatic Scene.* Krumb considers for a while the problem of whether to use one or two tables. He decides on one. With two blocks he builds a wall, puts the red racer at an angle of 45° toward it and then makes a small opening in it. Then he puts the father into the house so that the red racer, if driven, would run through the hole in the house and hit the father in the back. (Figure 15.) After this his doubts disappear. He obviously gets a funny idea and, laughing, puts the son and the maid together into a bed. The scene is completed quickly as seen in Figure 15. The father finds the son in bed with the maid and forbids intercourse. "Nothing homosexual is going on in the other room", adds the subject. The little girl is caught between two cars and the red racer speeding dangerously around the corner means one more danger for her. He seems not quite sure about which is the front and which the back of the racer, so that in reality it would, if "speeding dangerously" hit door and father.

2. *Comments:* This subject, the only one to put a boy and girl in a bed together, is a manifest homosexual—a fact which without any help from the rich but disorganized and complicated material of his life history, makes it possible for us to understand the meaning of the almost topological description of his inner conflicts in his scene; the living between two alternatives, both dangerous.

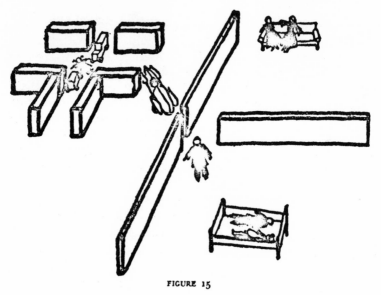

FIGURE 15

"Last year I had affairs with about three women and some fifteen men. Now it is only with men that I can find happiness. Being homosexual makes it possible for me to repress sexual impulses (?). I wish I could repress my feelings of guilt also."

It seems that Krumb tries to appease his growing feeling of guilt by the following arrangement: the father, between two rooms with a couple of the same sex in one and a couple of heterosexual lovers in the other, turns to the latter and forbids what they are doing. Thus the father himself decides against heterosexuality. The subject assures us that "nothing homosexual" happens in the other room, without our asking. In fact, he did not even know whether or not we were informed of his sexual predilections. Neither did he know that he had given himself away in his very first move: the arrangement of the racer, the door and the father. Knowing how often a house symbolizes a body and a car the genitals, this first construction represented the form and mode of a homosexual act: intercourse per anum. (See Oriol's second construction.) His indecision, then, as to which direction the car is going (whether crashing into the father or into the already mutilated girl) represents the alternative to the homosexual choice: to be the aggressive or the passive, the sadistic or the masochistic, partner. Here again is a choice, in which guilt doubtless drives him into the masochistic part, as many of his remarks in other interviews indicate, i.e., "The moving picture, 'Death Takes a Holiday', made me in love with death."

We have to leave it to the reports on their biographies to emphasize the complicated psychological aspects of the struggle of conscience in the individual subjects. If we could report more examples it would be worthwhile to define and to compare the different ways in which a conflict of conscience appears in the preparatory period, with the outcome as represented in the final scene. In the succession of toys which the subjects take and refuse at the beginning, one notices a peculiar alternation of symbols of repressed (maid, etc.) and repressing forces (policeman, etc.). The street seems always to offer a welcome opportunity for shifting the problem to the impersonal. The subjects show all varieties of guilt-feelings from the anxiety of losing love and protection (i.e., in building harmonious scenes with the mother at the table and the maid at the stove—entirely forgetful of the instructions) to the fear of catastrophe (policeman regulating traffic and preventing accidents as the only "dramatic" element), to various forms of self-punishment. It is as if these subjects, in the slow tortuous process of civilized maturation, had to find a painfully individual substitute for that sacrifice of a tooth or other symbol, which "cruel" primitives in their puberty rites inflict uniformly and once and for all on the boys of their community.

Second Construction. One year after this construction (it

might be well to state here again that not one word of interpretation was given to the subjects) Krumb was again asked to
construct a scene. He immediately asked: "May *two* things
happen?", thus taking up again the dualism of the first construction. He builds first two houses, then one house with two
parts, two rooms in each part. Again males and females are
separated. The father, he says, has a homosexual crush on a
severely wounded soldier and is in the bathroom—while in the
street the red racer is wrecked by the green truck. "I have a
feeling," the subject remarks, "that I have repeated my last
construction. I struggled for three minutes to overcome the
feeling that I did the same thing. Then I did—and found that
I had expressed homosexuality this time, which it seems I could
avoid last time." Finally, Krumb gives a confirmation of our
first assumption, which no doubt to many readers seemed
hazardous, namely, that the small hole in the house of the
first construction symbolized the homosexually attacked rectum; the house of the second construction, again, and at the
same place, has a small hole. Krumb remarks about it: "The
house is badly built, *bad odors* come out of here."

III.

X: Vulner

This is the construction of the only subject to whom the
suggestion "dramatic scene" implied a scene on a stage.

During the *Preparatory Period* Vulner is very hesitant.
He takes the son first, then the father, but puts them back and
seems to think seriously. He accidentally drops the son, plays
with the policeman, in serious thought, head dropped forward.
Should he take the cow? No. Then he takes the son again
and acts quickly.

The *Dramatic Scene* represents the corner of a room. The
mother is sitting in a chair, the father stands in front of her.
In a doorway stand son and daughter.

"The head minister is handing in his resignation. The day
before he had talked with the queen about the question of the

crown prince's marriage to a commoner. He had decided against it. In the meantime he has learned that it is his daughter whom the prince wishes to marry." Asked what the outcome will be, the subject replies, as if he were finishing a fairy tale told to a child, "He will probably marry her."

Analytic Remark: The most interesting aspect of this "really dramatic" construction is that there is very little to say about it. The scene possibly contains some hints in regard to the subject's family situation; he has one sister, no brother. But essentially the scene is a dramatic cliché and does not suggest any detail of the subject's biography, except that his mother is a writer and that, as a boy he had often participated in dramatic plays.

IV. (Final Remarks)

Having asked our subjects for a dramatic scene, we find a product of traumatic tension; instead of tragedy we find accident.

Dramatic and traumatic moments have one psychological element in common. Both are events which transgress the boundaries of the human ego, the first in widening it beyond individuation, the second in nearly extinguishing it. In other words, in a truly dramatic moment the individual is confronted with a choice which may make him the heroic or tragic master of human fate in its eternal aspects; he is allowed one chance to overcome the bondage of gravity and repetition. The traumatic moment destroys individuation, chance and choice, and makes the individual the helpless victim of repetition compulsion.

To be sure, in offering the little toys for a dramatic task we probably asked our subjects to take a too difficult step from the ridiculous to the sublime. In offering play material we ourselves have provoked the spirit of infantile conflict, since play "presupposes a psychic substance which is not quite structuralized yet".[1] The specific conflicts appearing in the constructions

[1] Robert Wälder *op. cit.*

indicate that the subjects when confronted with toys, continued where they had left off in their childhood play with the attempt to overcome traumatic experience by active repetition in play.

In describing these results we naturally do not characterize individuals in their conscious and rational individuation. The psychoanalytic microscope first focuses on neurotic material in its specific psychosexual characteristics. It shows us the inner frontier where the rational human mind—whether in the state of infancy, savagery or civilization—is constantly faced by the wilderness of the irrational.

The set-up of this particular study is not of any general value and is not recommended as a psychological experiment. But the results of this accidental undertaking may be of some interest in regard to the psychology and the psychopathology of play (important for the treatment of patients who cannot or do not want to speak): we can observe directly the structuralization of a given space in accordance with the qualities of a traumatic configuration, which imposes on the subjects' autoplastic and alloplastic behavior spatial elements of a past event or of the way in which the subject has armed himself against the (irrational) danger of its recurrence.

Further deciphering of play hieroglyphs—especially in the legitimate sphere of childhood—may offer valuable keys for the understanding of the prelinguistic and alinguistic strata of the human mind.

STUDIES IN THE INTERPRETATION OF PLAY:
I. CLINICAL OBSERVATION OF PLAY DISRUP-
TION IN YOUNG CHILDREN

ERIK HOMBURGER ERIKSON

Published as a separate and in *Genetic Psychology Monographs*, 1940, **22,**
557-671.

STUDIES IN THE INTERPRETATION OF PLAY: I. CLINICAL OBSERVATION OF PLAY DISRUPTION IN YOUNG CHILDREN*

ERIK HOMBURGER ERIKSON

Institute of Human Relations and School of Medicine, Yale University, New Haven, Connecticut

*Received in the Editorial Office on May 7, 1940, and published at Provincetown, Massachusetts. Copyright by The Journal Press.

These studies and their publication were aided by a grant to the Institute of Human Relations, Yale University, from the Josiah Macy, Jr. Foundation.

I. ORIENTATION

The purpose of this monograph is a modest and elementary one. Specimens of a psychotherapist's experience, namely, the observation of the first play enacted by young patients in his office, are reviewed, as it were, in slow motion. Two aspects are isolated as far as clinical material permits: What, to this psychotherapist, are the outstanding attributes of a play observation? What conscious considerations lead him to the "meaning" on which he bases his first diagnostic decisions?

This primitive inquiry marked the initial phase of a study of neurotic episodes and incipient neuroses in the pre-school child.[1] Unfortunately, however, simple purpose does not necessarily make for simple reading; and the concentration on small specimens in a field with such vast connotations and (recently) such general appeal necessitates a rather general introduction.

1.

The problem of play lies at the intersection of a variety of educational and clinical interests. In reaction to an era which hoped to develop virtues in children by clipping the wings of their spontaneity, modern education wishes to develop and to preserve, modern psychotherapy to utilize the benevolent powers which are said to emanate from the child's "creative" activities.

The contribution of psychoanalysis to this development is a singular one. It not only assumes, with others, a vague—self-teaching, self-healing—function in play, it also detects a detailed correspondence between central personality problems and both the content and the form of individual play creations.

The clinical psychoanalysis of play, however, has shared the

---

[1] The members of the Study Group were Felice Begg-Emery, M.D.; E. H. Erikson; Edith B. Jackson, M.D.; Marion C. Putnam, M.D., in the Department of Psychiatry and Mental Hygiene: and Ruth W. Washburn, Ph.D., in the Department of Child Development, Institute of Human Relations and School of Medicine, Yale University.

methodological limits of other psychoanalytic media with which Freud did not concern himself in detail (as he did with dreams, slips, witticisms, etc.). Their discernible phantasy content is welcome as something vaguely similar to and therefore useful substitutions for memories, dreams, and other media which are not plentiful in contacts with a small child; their *specific variables,* however, (such as, in play, the variables of extension in actual space) have not been considered worth any special methodological consideration. Responsibility for this neglect seems to lie in the same general attitude among psychoanalysts, which induced Freud to complain in regard to the interpretation of dreams, the oldest *via regia* to the human mind: *"Die Analytiker benehmen sich als wäre die Traumlehre abgeschlossen"* (7).

Tenaciously as the clinical worker may cling to standardized habits of interpretations and may try to see by means of a new medium only that which he had learned to see through older ones, his experience is never the same; new variables of changed experience constantly force him to imply new concepts or a different use of old ones. The clinical observer not only shares a particularly elusive *personal* equation with all those who observe with the naked eye and ear. His work also underlies the *practical* equation derived from the necessity to influence sooner or later the very material under observation. Finally, something like a *cultural* equation expresses the influence on his work and thought of his constantly changing function in science and society. Whatever scientific ore, therefore, may be present in the clinical experience (made elusive by technical, personal, practical, and cultural changes) comes to light mainly through the therapist's constant *efforts at making explicit some of the implicit (preconscious) steps of selecting, associating, and reasoning* which constitute his clinical "intuition" at a given time and in a given technique.

This being our object, we shall be forced to risk tiring the reader with details; details which will seem superfluous to the play technician whose optimism is satisfied with short cuts, and senseless to the psychoanalyst who has learned to view pessimistically any attempts at demonstrating psychoanalytic experience to the "outer world."

2.

In adult life (10) *"talking it out"* is the simplest autotherapeutic measure employed during tense periods by individuals who are not too asocial. Religious and psychiatric sects ritualize it in varying degrees by providing at regular intervals an authoritatively sanctioned listener who gives undivided attention and, sworn to neither censure nor betray, bestows absolution by explaining the individual's problem as belonging in a greater religious, ethical, sociological, medical context. The method finds its limitations where the clinical situation loses the detachment in which life can mirror itself and becomes the center of a passionate conflict as expressed in a too dependent (if not sexual) or too hostile attitude toward the therapist. In psychoanalytic terms: the limitation is set by the tendency (especially strong in neurotics) to superimpose one's basic conflicts on every new situation, even the therapeutic one. This leads to a *transference* which temporarily makes the therapeutic situation a disturbing factor in the patient's life. The patient is in resistance; in a war to end all wars, be becomes more deeply embroiled than ever. At this point non-psychoanalytic efforts are given up; the patient, it is said, does not want to get well or is too inferior to comprehend his obligations in treatment. Therapeutic psychoanalysis at this point systematically begins to make use of the knowledge that no neurotic is undivided in his wish to get well and by necessity transfers his dependencies and hostilities to the treatment and the person of the therapist; in revealing these "resistances" he points the way to *his* treatment.

"To play it out" is the most natural autotherapeutic measure childhood affords. Whatever other rôle play may have in the child's development (and I do not think that these rôles are adequately known), the child also uses it to make up for defeats, sufferings, and frustrations, especially those resulting from a technically and culturally limited use of language. This, the "cathartic" theory of play is one of the many play theories, all of which agree only in assuming an untimely tension. If not a *catharsis* for excessive (traumatic) stimulation in the past, play is considered the expression of a *surplus energy* for which there is no more "practical" use at the moment; with untimeliness projected into phylogenetic dimensions, play becomes a *recapitulation* of (now useless) phylogenetic

leftovers or the *preparatory* expression of what in the future will be useful activity.

In Spencer's classic words, wherever circumstances allow or suggest play, those tendencies are *"simulated"* which are *"unusually ready to act, unusually ready to have their correlative feelings aroused"* (14), (but at the same time are *not any more* or *not as yet practicable* in connection with their real goal).

Of all organisms the human child is probably the one who has to learn to postpone temporarily and permanently the most formidable array of tendencies which because of his slow maturation and his higher aspirations are precocious or definitely out of place. Some of them (as Freud has recognized in neurotics) remain "unusually ready to have their correlative feelings aroused" throughout life. Our new knowledge of such unconscious and subverbal "readinesses" gives the previous theories of play a new and specifically human meaning. In all its slow maturation and long defenselessness, the human child, so we learn, lives through periods of diffuse, culturally and biologically impracticable impulses of a sensual and aggressive nature, which he cannot help attaching to the narrow circle of his very originators, protectors, and educators—his family. The task of maturation, then, is to outgrow in the most constructive manner these premature emotional and instinctual attachments while outgrowing the need for protection. But this is a slow and partly indefinite process; and the human animal not only plays most and longest, it also remains ready to become deadly serious in the most irrational contexts.

Modern play therapy is based on the observation that a child made ambivalent and insecure by a secret hate against or fear of the natural protectors of his play (family, neighborhood) seems able to use the protective sanction of an understanding adult, in professional elaboration the play therapist, to regain some play peace. The most obvious reason is that the child has the toys and the adult for himself, sibling rivalry, parental nagging, and routine interruptions do not disturb the unfolding of his play intentions, whatever they may be.

The observing adult's "understanding" of such play, then, is a beneficial factor even where it finds only an intangible minimum of expression in the child's presence, while its value for an indirect use in advice and guidance can hardly be over-estimated. The peace provided by solitary play or by play in the presence of a sympathetic adult often radiates for some time, often long and intensively enough to meet the radiation of recognition and love from some source in the environment, a necessary factor in all· psychological cures. The chances therefore seem better where the mother too has an opportunity to relieve in conversations her ambivalence toward the child and is prepared to respond to his improvement.

As we shall demonstrate, however, the phenomenon of *transference* in the work with the playing child, as well as with the verbalizing adult, marks the point where simple measures fail, namely, when an emotion of such intensity as to defeat playfulness forces an immediate and only thinly-veiled discharge into the play and into the relationship to the play observer. The failure is characterized by what is to be described in this monograph as *play disruption*, i.e., the sudden and complete or diffused and slowly spreading inability to play.

Recent work in this country has emphasized the alternatives of "passivity" or "activity" on the part of the play observer, the extreme passive attitude representing a certain seductive lifelessness, a kind of play hostess attitude, the extreme active one an animated encouragement of the child to "release aggression" against toys named after members of the child's family. Where a child can follow this latter suggestion without immediate or delayed play disruption we have no reason to be worried about the child, although the "release" theory implied in such procedures seems tenable only in clearly "traumatic" cases and there only theoretically, as the thorough analysis of such cases shows. The clinical problem seems to be solved only by the establishment of permanent and sufficient every day release channels and not by a momentary release under special conditions. Much of this "release" ideology as well as certain forms of purely symbolic and purely sexual interpretation seem to be a revival of the most primitive techniques of the early psychoanalysis of adults—now transferred to the new field of play therapy.

Those children who transfer not the solution but the insolvability of their problems into the play situation and onto the person of the observer need to be induced by *systematic interpretation* to reconsider, on a more verbal level, the constellations which have overwhelmed them in the past and are apt to overwhelm them when re-occurring. Where *this* goal is given, child psychoanalysis begins.

Child analysis proper, in the cases which are its domain, seeks to provide the child with opportunity for catharsis only in the frame of an intimate therapeutic contact in which *repeated interpretation* furthers the *verbal communication* of inner dangers and the establishment of a *supremacy of conscious judgment* over unmanageable or incompletely repressed tendencies. To interpret means to reveal to the patient, at a *dynamically specific moment*, meanings which he can fully admit to himself only under the guidance of the therapist. Such interpretation is impossible without a technique which systematically and consistently reveals the *dynamics of the developing therapeutic situation,* especially the forces of transference and resistance. Its application is useless or dangerous where there is not time enough to follow the patient and to give new interpretations until a lasting ability is secured to express in a more conscious and social, more humorous and more useful manner that which he first could only admit to verbalization under the guidance of a therapist. Interpretation waits for a specific moment; it needs preparation and after-treatment; it does not claim success until a general and lasting increase of constructive vitality seems secured.

As the treatment proceeds and as the child's verbal powers increase, play observation loses much if not most of its exclusive importance. For the age group reported, however, the investigation of the child's play is a natural first step which coincides with the first step of a variety of treatments; while it can be abandoned or deferred without damage, it can also be pursued and developed without break.

3.

As stated above, this monograph demonstrates the analytic method merely in so far as it permits one to locate through play observation the approximate "seat" and extent of an emotional disturbance before definite clinical procedure is decided upon. This procedure may or may not be child psychoanalysis. Only in the last case to be reported will an effort be made to demonstrate the function of therapeutic interpretations. I should like however, at least in the introduction, to transgress the scope of this monograph and to indicate briefly some views in regard to the wider problem of psychoanalysis.

Psychoanalysis, besides being a psychotherapeutic method, is a method of research, a system of psychological and "metapsychological" concepts and a social phenomenon. It rests on observation, on speculation, and on professional organization.

Freud's unconventional eye gave *clinical observation* a new focus and a new scope. The new focus was neurotic man at the intersection of nature and culture, the scope so vast that the neurologist Freud, in conceptualizing the peculiar logic of a neurosis, found himself referring to such seemingly and academically remote phenomena as the primitive's superstition, the child's wishes, the artist's imagination. However, in doing so Freud painstakingly emphasized the fact that the everyday basis of his expanding system was and remained the observation of the forces most clearly operating in the clinical situation; namely, transference, resistance, repression, regression, etc. The clinical observer of a verbalizing adult sees his personality outlined in the way in which his feelings, memories, hopes, etc., do or do not cross the threshold of verbalization, once this threshold is emphasized by the suggestion to associate freely. He has to evaluate a *dynamic scale* of representations, on which a single idea or complex of ideas alternately appears remembered, re-enacted, dreamt, avoided, projected on others, repudiated, joked about, etc., each time with specific *disguises* and *omissions* and accompanied by a *specific quantity and quality of awareness*.

Psychoanalysis emphasizes the fact that the non-clinical fields such as psychology, anthropology, child development, etc., overlap one another precisely in as far as they are psychological. This could be demonstrated either by a changing of focus of their own methods, which would make it possible to find in their material 'the facts which Freud found in his neurotics, or by an adaptation of the psychoanalytic method to their material, i.e., through methods which use in these non-clinical situations whatever forces in them correspond to the clinical forces of resistance, regression, and transference.[2]

Thus one will see how individuals and groups defend themselves

---

[2]For example, the anthropological observer with psychoanalytic training learns to understand, one is tempted to say, the culturality of a cultural

against ideas and needs which are considered dangerous to the commanding ideas and needs of their reality, and how the *suppressed, the expressed, and the aspired to are interwoven.*

In the application of psychoanalysis to the study of children, the variations in the individual's quantity and quality of verbalized awareness obviously cannot provide the proper dynamic scale because children, on the whole, cannot obey the rule of free association. Of the scales to be applied instead, two will be elaborated in this monograph, namely, the correlation of the individual's *verbal* behavior with his *spatial* expression and his recognizable changes of *affect.*[3]

There are a number of facts which, for better or worse, are constantly re-established by daily psychoanalytic experience: the discrepancy between the representation in verbalized consciousness and the motivating power of certain ideas (repression); the priority among these ideas of those concerning the child's first bodily (sexual) orientation in the world of physical and social facts; their disguised expression in various metaphoric ways; the sexual deficiencies and the defensive personality changes resulting from them, etc. All these facts are taken for granted here although they are, of course, considered subject to further scientific observation. The observation of these facts, however, and the theory of transference, resistance, and repression implies and has led to many concepts of what Freud calls "metapsychological" nature.

Freud and the first psychoanalysts were faced with the task of conceptualizing a field which had almost no tradition. They were erudite men who had at their disposal modes of thought from a variety of the scientific and extrascientific fields which in the past had monopolized man's conduct, such as theology, philosophy, and art. In the psychoanalytic system not only the superficial evidence

---

entity from the way a given complex of ideas is represented on the dynamic scale of a culture's collective consciousness: in one variation as historical memory and in another as mythological history; in one disguise re-enacted in heavy rituals, in another in light games; in a third entirely represented by avoidance. The complex may be recognizable in culture pattern dreams or in individual dreams; in humorous or in hateful projections on the neighbor, on the prehuman race, or on the animal world; it may be represented in deviating behavior designating either the select or the damned or both.

[3] A future psychoanalysis of play will be based on material allowing the weighing of an individual's play against that of his age and culture group.

of an occasional term such as *Oedipus Complex* points into the past, but, more important, such sweeping conceptual configurations as the free floating in the body of a *libido* with its *cathexis* and *catharsis;* in the mind, the struggle of an ego between an *id* and a *superego;* and in the world at large, a gigantic melting of life and death instincts.

The libido concept, for example, might be suspected of having fallen heir to the Greek interpretation of hysteria; there the *uterus* wandered about in the body, selecting its organ for interference. In Freud's system it is not the uterus but the *libidinal cathexis of the psychic representation of the genitals* which is displaced to the representation of other parts of the body which then show conversion symptoms. The same libido, if cathexing the therapist's representation in the patient's mind (and reinforced by the transference of the cathexis of the father image to that of the therapist's) creates the favorable condition for the influence of the therapist on the patient, as the *animal spirits* of the last century did while still actually crossing the space between patient and therapist.

In spite of his antiphilosophic sentiments, Freud on occasion referred, not without sovereign pleasure, to such similarities between his concepts and those of prepsychological thinkers, the last example being the identity of the *life and death instincts* with Empedocles' *philia* and *veikos* (7). His *"id"* he early recognized as a kin of Schopenhauer's *will.* Both *id* and *will,* several steps further back in the history of conceptual configurations, take on personal shape, appear as the *devil.*

Freud has traced these and many other ancient images from their projection onto the periphery of man's world back to where they originated, in *man's mind,* where observed with dynamic tools they become a subject of psychology. He draws these images closer to the scientific thinking of his day (and nearer to observation and, ultimately, experiment) by making them *quantitative* and *genetic.* Thus, the libido theory on the one hand becomes something like a theory of *preservation of psychic energy;* on the other hand, the theory of the fate of the libido directly contacts the *theory of evolution.*

Freud's historical habit of weighting a particular observation with whatever standard of conceptualization seemed adequate to further its clarification, has led to the use in psychoanalytic literature of a disturbing variety of, as it were, terminological currencies which alternately represent human data in terms of the mythology of milleniums, the philosophy of centuries, and the scientific methods of decades. Freud implies that in time all these currencies will be exchanged, at their face value, into one based on the clinical and experimental standard of the day.

The real danger, however, of the pre-scientific ancestry of revolutionary thought in psychology has proved to be and will, at least for a while, be a group-psychological one. A certain idea, by fitting into an ancient, possibly long-suppressed mode of thought, to some appears immediately convincing and pertaining to the nature of the experience: "this I have always known." The same mode of thought being alien (perhaps repressed) to others, may deter them from consideration of the same idea even if it is already well on its way to substantiation: "this I have always avoided." In such development observation is often little consulted; group identification replaces scientific method; and a regression takes place to conflicts in ancestral thinking and to spritual and philosophic leftovers and leftouts.

This third influence in the formation of a system, namely, the group psychological meaning derived from the organization of its adherents, has been especially powerful in the history of psychoanalysis for another reason intrinsic in its nature.

When Freud, in the good faith of scientific ethos, first revealed the hitherto undescribed manifestation on which he focused his attention, and the unheard of selections and associations of his mind which made him focus on them, he was met with an overwhelmingly ugly response from the scientists of his day. Partially understandable as a Victorian reaction against a bold mind and his sovereign habits of deduction, this response nevertheless had certain qualities in common with the behavior and the argumentation of a cornered patient: it forced Freud to realize that his era was going to resist as one patient the Freudian kind of enlightenment. He proceeded, however, to recognize and to conceptualize this *"resistance" as an attribute of living psychological matter*. Freud's observations had struck at the specific illusion which had reached its climax in his era, namely, that there was no psychological limit to the subordination of sex and aggression to will, belief, and reason. Resistance, in the larger sense, is human inability to accept any theory which makes the current conception of "free will" relative.

The ever-renewed detection and therapeutic utilization of the selective, repressive, projective mechanisms in the human mind are the tools which Freud gave to psychotherapy and psychology; they point beyond systems and schools for they insist on pursuing resistance wherever it chooses to hide in the evolution of human consciousness, and no school can avoid for long becoming a hiding place for collective regressions—not even the psychoanalytic one from which groups of adherents necessarily aim to derive a secondary gain by ascribing to themselves more than a relative freedom from resistance and privileges such as methodological isolation.

But there is no reason to doubt that all these phenomena will gradually and permanently become subject to the developing psychoanalytic method itself. Always proceeding along the line of most resistance, it will stimulate clinical observation and its application, and will make it possible to understand conceptual and group psychological processes such as marked the beginning of its own history.

4.

Freud has not analyzed children himself. He based the reconstruction of psychosexual development in childhood on the systematic analysis of the verbalizations of adult neurotics and on a wealth of corroboratory, although unsystematic, observations of childhood. When it became apparent that clinical contact with small children was possible, Freud left this field to others (and expressly to his women pupils). The few references to direct child observation to be found in his work (8) make apparent the loss which this Victorian fact implies for child psychology.

Anna Freud's cautious and clear *"Introduction to the Technique of Child Analysis"* (5) still seems to be the only safe technical statement in regard to the application of psychoanalysis to clinical work with children. However, detailed discussions of her Vienna seminar, which represented the most significant expansion of her basic technical ideas, have not been published. The field has thus been left to clinical abstracts and to one most ambitious systematic attempt, namely, Melanie Klein's *"The Psychoanalysis of Children"* (11).

Mrs. Klein has enriched our thinking by concentrating on some neglected features of infantile, and especially female, fantasy life,

such as the preoccupation with the body interior. Her book, however, abounds in methodologically irresponsible statements referring
to what its author is supposed to have "shown" in regard to the
psychology of normal childhood. From these "demonstrations" she
and her followers derive the license not only to reconstruct earliest
psychic development where it is least approachable, but also to
convey such reconstructions to child patients. Their interpretations,
fairy tales stripped of all artistry, seem to fascinate children and
are said to cure them. The author of this paper cannot, at the
present time, overcome a suspicion as to the final adaptation of the
child cured by this method to any environment, except that which
cultivates a special type of psychoanalytic outlook.[4]

In some of the contributions to the child analysis number of the
Psychoanalytic Quarterly (1), a new living relationship between
disturbed child and understanding adult (a kind of doctor-aunt who
helps the child to find words for unspeakable experiences) is lucidly
described.[5] As far as smaller children are concerned, such descrip-
tions seem most convincing where the historical tool of psychoanalysis, namely, "making conscious," is not assumed a priori to have
been applied. While the concepts of resistance and transference
when applied to smaller children lose little of their value as tools
of investigation, repression, because of the lack of dependable verbal
contact between therapist and child, becomes a somewhat meaningless concept; by inferring it, one often misses the opportunity to
observe stages in which what is later to be called repression is just
about to happen, and by treatment seems prevented rather than made
retroactive. It is exactly this prevention of a disastrous gap between
verbal and subverbal experiences in childhood which promises to
become the most useful contribution of psychoanalysis to a future
era (and promises to have been the most poignant criticism of the
passing one).

However, we have not always been conscious enough of the fact
that in the humanities premature reconstruction has to resort to
medieval images. In some of our writings Freud's tentative ab-
stractions of a topology, a genetics, and a mechanics of psychic life

---

[4]For the most comprehensive criticism of the "English School of Child
Analysis" see Robert Waelder (16).

[5]The author wishes to recommend especially the papers by Bertha Bornstein and Steff Bornstein (1).

are inadvertently colored by visions and clothed in moods. What the child's ego is said to experience and to do often goes even beyond the concept of a persona in a person; it implies an organism with a sensory and motor system of its own within the organism—indeed, a human-like being between a devil- and a god-like one. Like *diaboli* of old, these parts of the psyche reflect and act, avoid effort and gain satisfaction with sly and dialectic skill. Similarly, in the conceptualization of inaccessible parts of childhood there occur *homunculi* of synthetic babies who are complete miniature editions of adult cannibals or psychotics; or reconstructed newborns laden with *primordial images* of sin and guilt. Thus, residues of the intellectual past and by-products of extra-scientific ideologies of today are used to draw prematurely into a developmental synthesis of "the child," striking observations as well as moods, beliefs, and divinations from many planes.

Any description of a prolonged period of child psychoanalytic treatment seems to find a powerful obstacle in the fact that the child, relatively more than the adult, is contantly changing under the influence of extratherapeutic factors. Therapeutic influences act at best as accelerators and inhibitors on a continuum of maturational processes which, *in their normal or, let us say, extra-clinical manifestations, for the most part have never been properly studied and described.* The intimate changes observed during a child's treatment therefore are too easily explained as a function of the treatment; while the danger implied in attempts to influence by means derived from clinical work the as yet unknown factors in the maturation of the child must be obvious. Thus the early possibility of basing a reconstruction of the child's normal inner development on present clinical data and applying such premature syntheses to the philosophy and practice of education, seems doubtful. But it will be as rewarding as it is time-consuming to apply child-psychopathological knowledge to research in "normal" childhood, i.e., the development and inner life of children whom neurosis has not isolated from the supporting field of group values.

II. THE INITIAL SITUATION AND ITS ALTERNATIVES

1.

Every psychotherapist has certain vague expectations in regard to what a disturbed child entering his room for the first time may be expecting of him and may do. Against this generalized picture the behavior of a single child stands out in its dramatic individuality.

Our young patient usually arrives hand in hand with his mother. He can be expected to have made a mental note of the fact that our office is in a "hospital-like" institution. On entering the waiting room he finds a friendly secretary and is then invited into an inner room about half of which (signified by "adult furniture") is set aside for the therapist's plainly non-medical business, the other half (signified by floor space and an array of ordinary toys) for a child's play. He is told sooner or later that he is expected to let his mother withdraw to the waiting room and to allow the connecting door to be closed; the therapist and the toys are then to be at his disposal.

This situation confronts the young patient with a maze of conflicting possibilities. We would like to describe it as consisting of several overlapping fields of ambiguity which are created by the child's relation to mother, therapist, toys, and inner conflict.

There is first of all his *mother*. He may hold on to her hand or body, insist on staying with her in the waiting room, demand that the door remain open, or stubbornly remain near the door which has closed between her and him. If he does this, the situation is for him still related mainly to one goal, his mother, and through her the way home from a vague danger. This idea, however, is rarely unequivocally pleasant. Our small patient usually has reached a deadlock with his mother, who cannot understand why he does not "simply drop" his problem; while the home atmosphere, in which he, in most cases, has been subjected to varying educational methods, has become charged with unsolved conflicts. Thus, frightened as he may be, he feels attracted by the *doctor possibilities,* the second field, and one which offers possible escape from the unbearable pressure of the domestic situation. Something which the mother or somebody else has said usually has created a slight hope in the child that the therapist may be a person who understands the conditions and the tempo in which a symptom of fear can be gradually abandoned without giving place to chaos within or more trouble without. Many a child has learned also to expect that he will be able to play for time by repeating to this new therapist what has satisfied the old ones. On the other hand the therapist has been called a "doctor" and the medical implications of the surroundings add to the mere strangeness of the situation and create the expectation in the child that some kind of surprise attack is to be made on his physical or moral inviolacy. The mother, with the best intentions, often transfers the negative aspects of the "mother field" into the field of doctor possibilities; she insists, for example, on reporting in the child's presence latest developments, on admonishing, or even threatening him, or on trying to secure the therapist's promise of diagnosis and advice. Literally and psychologically, therefore, the mother has to be referred to the waiting room; the child must feel that time has another quality in the doctor sphere, in which, paradoxically, there is no hurry about getting well.

In the meantime, a third ambiguous field[6] has competed with mother and therapist in dominating the child's expectancies, namely the *toys*.[7] For the child they open another haven, in which space too has another quality, and the therapist usually is quite glad to resign for a while in favor of this quasi-free sphere. Indeed, *"what would we do without toys,"* has become a common exclamation now that we have relaxed our efforts to ignore this most natural tool. The toys evoke in the child that remainder of playful explorativeness which his neurosis and the present doctor situation has not been able to submerge; and once he has started to select and manipulate, we can be sure that the temptation to play and to be the unquestioned and inviolable master in a microcosmic sphere will be great. However, we again see the child manifest hesitation. He has experienced too often the fact that the imagined omnipotence in the toy world only makes him feel his impotence the more keenly when he is suddenly interrupted. Playfulness does not rule until

---

[6]I must acknowledge here the influence of Kurt Lewin's terminology, although my grasp of it does not seem to go beyond the recognition of a most valuable reformulation which gives certain modern modes of thinking terminological recognition.

[7]In regard to the influence of the presence of these toys on the total situation, an animal psychologist's remark comes to my mind: "Whenever a rat is placed within sight or smell of food, it appears quite obvious and therefore it tends to remain unremarked that his selectiveness as to the surrounding means-objects .are thereby affected" (15).

(and then only as long as) pressing purposes and fears have lost their compelling power. Thus the child often begins to play with hesitation, with selection, with one eye on the therapist or the door—but he begins to play.

Peace seems to reign. The mother is comfortably seated in the waiting room and has promised "not to go away"; the doctor has been diagnosed as a person who will not make surprise attacks on one's bodily or moral reserve; the toys, sure not to question or to admonish, promise a time of "unpurposeful" play.

However, it is at this point that the most dangerous field of ambiguity; namely, the child's reluctance to confess and his need to communicate his *conflict,* takes possession of the peaceful situation. Whatever it is that drives the child—an urge to get rid of some past or to prepare himself for some future, or both—the ever-present gestalt of the life task which has proved too much for him appears in the metaphoric representation of the microsphere. It is here that our "sign-reading" sets in, and that the tools which Freud gave us become indispensable; for they make us realize that in the playful arrangement which the child is driven to superimpose on the inventory of toys we offer him, he offers us an outline of the "inner maze" in which he is caught. Our small patients either show an anxious care in excluding this or that toy from their play or they work themselves toward a borderline where they themselves suddenly find their own doings unsafe, not permissible, unworkable, or unsatisfactory to the point of extreme discomfort. They cannot go on playing in peace—a phenomenon which we shall call play disruption.

I shall give a brief example of the place of such a play disruption in the four fields of ambiguity, governed as they are by the changing valences of the parent who is present, the therapist, the toys, and the shadow of inner conflict.

A girl of four still withstands toilet training. When put on the toilet, she seems unable to "let go"; later she soils her bed. Recently she was knocked down by an automobile; this has increased her inaccessibility and her pale stubbornness. [As is obvious from her utterances at home, a small neighborhood dog is, at the moment, important in her fantasy life. It is female like herself, and not housebroken, and recently was knocked down by an automobile too; but unlike herself, it is frequently beaten for soiling, was badly hurt in the accident (it lost a leg). This little dog apparently represents to her all that "is coming to her."]

Very pale, the little girl has finally left her mother in the waiting room. She stands near the door of my room, sucking her finger, neither willing to play nor wanting to go back to her mother. I try to help her by outlining with some blocks a few rooms on the floor (an approach I use only on rare occasions). A little girl lies in a bed, and a woman stands in the middle of the bedroom from which a door leads into a bathroom. There is a garage with a car and a man. After a while the little girl suddenly warms up, approaches with flushed cheeks and kicks the woman doll so that it falls over, closes the bathroom door and goes to the toy shelf to get three shiny red cars for the man in the garage. May we say she expresses a dislike for what must mean to her a mother in front of the little girl's bed and for the demand of the open bathroom door; and that she shows a readiness to give whatever the cars mean to the man (father). At this point, however, she bursts into tears and anxiously asks, *"Where is my mummy?"* In panicky haste she takes three red pencils from my desk and runs out of the room to present them to her mother. Then she sits down beside her, pale and rigid, determined not to return to me. (The mother wants to give back the pencils, but she is told that the child is free to return them another time.)

The patient has scarcely reached home when she seems to feel guilty about having taken my pencils and shows signs of despair at not being able to bring them back until the next day. However, when the time for her next hour has arrived, she sits in the waiting room clutching the pencils in one hand, some unknown object in the other. She refuses to come with me. After a while it becomes noticeable that she has soiled herself. When she is picked up to be led to the bathroom, the pencils fall to the floor and with them a little toy dog, one of whose legs has been broken off.

If we undertake to interpret this example properly, we would be led to consider in detail the patterns of guilt-feeling in this child: Having manifested aggression toward the woman in the play setup, she experienced the fear of the possible loss of her mother's love; in hurrying to bring her an equivalent of what she had given to the man in the play, she happened to snatch objects which belonged to me, thus provoking a situation which would again ask for acts of rectification and which would imply an element of desire for punishment. (As if under compulsion to do or to allude to that which brings punishment, she held on to my property, brought the toy dog with a damage identical with her dog friend's injury, and soiled in my room—transferring a "symptom" for which she had never been punished in a way either quantitatively or qualitatively equal to the hostility it expressed, as subsequently became apparent.)

What interests us here first of all is the traffic between the fields outlined above and the play disruption's place in them. The little girl moderately sure that her mother would not leave and somewhat loosened by the playful way in which the therapist approached her problem got as far as to say in the language of play signs that she did not like the idea of the lady standing there near the open bathroom door but was willing to give the reddest cars to the man, when she must have experienced what Adam did when he heard God's voice: *"Adam, where art thou?"* Her play suddenly seemed all-visible in the mother-field and she went to atone for her deed not, however, without stealing my pencils and thus innocently establishing a new goal in the doctor sphere. The trip home again increased the stubbornness against mother and bathroom demands and, consequently, the importance of the goal she had established in my sphere. The next day, back in my office and faced with the necessity and possibility of making everything come out even, she is caught by emotional paralysis and her symptom expresses for her what she did not dare to express in her play; namely, the inability "to give" to an ambivalently loved person.

It is this very inability which in this case called for analysis and re-education. However, we shall have to resist the temptation to describe the little girl's treatment at this point. Instead we concentrate on some further aspects of the described play situation.

2.

We may call the toy scene on the floor *microcosmic*, i.e., *an arrangement of small objects in such a way that their configuration signifies a configuration of conflicting forces in the child's life*, in this case the child's retentive attitude toward her mother and her generous attitude toward the father. That the woman in the play really signified her mother (and that the man, perhaps, already indicated a father transference on the therapist) became plain when the microcosmic play was disrupted and she tried to rearrange another sphere in such a way that it represented a reversal of the "guilty" microcosmic configuration: she gave to her mother—and robbed me. Such *rearrangements of the child's relationship to the real persons or the life-sized objects present in the therapeutic situation* we shall designate as *macrocosmic*. In this case the traffic from what we shall call, for short, the *microsphere* to the *macrosphere* implied a play disruption which, of course, is not always necessarily the case. Such a shift can take place as a playful expansion, perhaps with a transition from solitary play to a game, especially if another person is induced to play a rôle in the desired macrocosmic arrangement. (Using, for example, with an omnipotent gesture, a chair for a horse to ride on and to order about, would be the macrocosmic play equivalent to the microcosmic form of making a toy rider hop along the floor.)

Beside the microcosmic and macrocosmic "spheres" of representation we can discern an autocosmic one: *the sphere of dramatization by means of an interplay of body parts and organ systems.* The little girl's soiling belongs here: it was a *symptom in the autosphere.* There is also *autocosmic play,* i.e., the original play in the growing world of the child's expanding body consciousness and the mutual enchantment of its parts.

3.

The antithesis of play disruption is a phenomenon which we shall call "play satiation." If play "succeeds," i.e., if it is not disrupted from within or interrupted from without, it has an effect on the child comparable to a few hours of good, long-needed sleep—everything "looks different." I do not doubt that it is this autotherapeutic function of play which we are restoring in many cases by creating for a child regular and undisturbed periods of play, no matter how we rationalize what is happening during such a "cure." In contrast to the little girl's macrocosmic outbreak after the microcosmic disruption we sometimes see microcosmic play satiation lead directly into a macrocosmic play or game in which the rearrangement achieved in small dimensions is tried out (and this often too courageously for the child's own anxiety) on big objects and people. I shall give here a non-psychiatric example of this normal phenomenon.

I once visited a boy of four a few hours after he had undergone an ear operation. He was, of course, most uncomfortable, insisted that many parts of his body hurt and that he wanted to urinate and defecate but was unable to do so. Three questions were most apparent in his complaints: first, whether or not the doctors were going to stick more instruments into him; second, why it was that only the doctor could remove the bandage around his head; third, whether his ear was still under the bandage.[8]

An understanding doctor had given him a roll of adhesive tape shortly before and he had held it, clutched in his hand, ever since. The tape was wouna on a tin spool which fitted into a tin cylinder. Only one end of the spool could be inserted into the cylinder because the rim on the other end extended beyond the cylinder and served to fasten the two pieces together. The boy removed the spool from its container and suggested the following play: "You try to put this (A) into that (B)" (Figure 1). Accidentally I tried it the wrong way,[9] whereupon he said with startling emphasis,

A B

FIGURE 1

---

[8]Worries of this type are, of course, common among hospitalized children. The increased specialization which makes it necessary that before and after an operation the child is contacted by a great number of experts, each of whom has his own little method of "talking the child's language," brings with it a disturbing variety of assurances, reassurances, promises, back-slaps, playful threats, etc., which may often make the psychological safety a reverse function of the physiological one said to be achieved by the specialistic perfection. As our patient was being prepared for his operation one attending individual had referred to his "beautiful eyelashes" and jokingly threatened that upon waking up he would find them removed from his eyes and attached to hers.

[9]That he had the spool and that I made a mistake have to be considered as (regularly present) *supporting factors* in the particular development of what, in view of its coherent manifestation, must be considered the "contemplated play configuration.

"It's much too big!" Since he kept repeating these words with a vague expression of pleasure, I coöperated by not accomplishing the deed, and by repeating my mistake over and over again, giving him the repeated opportunity to pronounce the magic phrase, *"It's much too big."* Each time I had failed to fit the spool and cylinder into one another, he took the two objects and, fitting them correctly said with much emphasis, *"Now it's closed."* The repetition of this ritual of pretending that *only he could stick A into B* already seemed to influence his general condition considerably.

Suddenly he said, *"Let's pretend this is a leg and it's sore."* He attempted to unwind the roll of adhesive tape, but found he could not separate the layers. Disappointed, he asked me to unwind it. I played that it was very difficult to unwind, whereupon he said with glee, *"We need a giant for that."* I pretended to phone the nurse to send up a giant, then left the room and reappeared as the giant. However, I had a white coat on which made the play situation resemble too much the actuality (he was a patient expecting a doctor). He asked anxiously why the giant had an apron on. He quickly recovered, however, and after the giant's initial help, began to remove the tape from the spool (to which task, as had now been proved, only a giant's strength was equal). Pieces of it were placed around the cylinder, which was now serving as the "leg."

There was much joyful concentration on the completion of the "bandage." But a few tiny spots of red inscription were not covered by the tape and he now concentrated on them. *"Look! There's a toe sticking out. And here is another toe, and another toe."* I asked, *"Shall we put the bandages around the toes, too?"* He replied enthusiastically, *"Yes,"* and put the tiny bandages over the toes. While doing so he began to sing and already felt quite cool. It was evident that he felt no pain.

When the entire surface of the cylinder was fully bandaged, the patient inserted the spool into it and taped over the whole configuration. *"Nobody can take this off."* He asked his mother and me to remove the bandage, but, of course, "we couldn't." Whereupon he proudly repeated that, first, *nobody but he could remove the bandage or the spool;* that, second, *he was not going to do it.* Our "requests" were of no avail.

It will already have become evident to the reader that the patient arranged the play objects in such a way that they expressed in sign magic his active mastery over the situation victimizing him at the time. That only he could stick Object *A* into Object *B*, a pleasure provided by the nature of the toy (which, as we shall see, was subsequently bandaged), may have had a quite general meaning of mastery, although it may have already implied the more specifically satisfying idea that nobody (i.e., the physicians) could stick more objects into his head. The fact that he was obliged to wait until the physician was willing to remove his bandage was reversed by the game wherein only a giant could remove the adhesive tape from the spool and only the child could remove the bandage from the cylinder (but would not do it). Finally, since he himself had covered the "toes" so carefully, he knew that these "extremities" were there and that he himself had covered them—an arrangement which might have been reversing the actual situation wherein the physician had covered his ears and would not allow him to see whether or not they were still there.

After approximately half an hour of such play the patient was smiling and singing. He fell asleep after I left. When he woke up again he smiled mischievously and said to his mother, who was sitting beside his bed, *"Let's put some bandage over the doctor's eyes when he comes in; let's put it all over him. The big bad wolf —only then we wouldn't have enough bandage left if Charlie[10] hurts his leg."*

Leaving aside the last "altruistic" remark in which the patient already visualized a time when he might be providing bandages for his brother (who had by then become the medical victim), we see in the remark about the doctor being covered all over by the bandage a *typical omnipotent rearrangement in phantasy of the macrosphere in accordance with a previous microcosmic rearrangement.* First, only the patient could make and remove bandages, and now the doctor himself becomes the victim of bandaging to a degree ("all over him") surpassing the discomfort he had created for the child.

This wishful and wilful restructuralization in play of the child's most immediate sphere of discomfort uses, of course, all the mechanisms which Freud showed were governing factors in play, in his classical example of a boy who had to adapt to his mother's absence:[11] the working over of an experience in which one had been a *passive*

---

[10]The patient's brother.
[11]The reader is urged to read this description and its discussion (8).

victim by its representation in such a way that one becomes the active aggressor against a toy or a partner. As for microcosmic play, the traumatic experience is caught in a *small* and *simple* configurational frame (an accessible *"Beutefeld"*), and is to be reprojected in its all-too-simple formulation into the bigger world, which consequently becomes a macrocosmic play-and-error field for microcosmic theories.

In the little girl's case the microsphere represented "a family"; in the case of the hospital patient, endangered parts of the body, ear, head, etc. Thus a variety of segments of the pressingly immediate life situation may be projected into this least refractory of all spheres of representation. A child concerned about "the body as a whole" or even about "life as a whole," may build corresponding configurations both as wishful arrangements and as traumatic repetitions. Illustrations of this will follow.

4.

Of special interest is one of the intermediate steps between the spheres of representation, namely, behavior with *extensions of the autosphere.* Play belongs in this category wherever it is clear that an isolated object is used as a means to extend or intensify the mode of expression of an organ or an organ-system and does not become a part of an extrabodily microcosmic arrangement. Let us say a block, if replacing the finger as an object of licking, is a part of an autocosmic extension; it would still be one if rhythmically banged against another block, while it would become a part of a microcosmic arrangement when, with consideration for its physical laws and its usual connotation, it is placed on another block so that together they may form a building.[12]

---

[12]A schizophrenic patient at the Worcester State Hospital was asked to build a house. He looked into space, grasped one block firmly and "tasted it" with his fingers; then he took a block in the other hand and did the same thing. With an expression of recognition, he bent his head forward, then brought first one then the other block to his mouth, snapping at them, making sounds of "tasting" and exclaiming "Good!", "Good!" He did not touch them with his lips; nor was he able to put more blocks on top of one another than the two which he could hold in his two hands. Similarly, when given toy cars, he could (with much delight) push them so that they flew over the edge of the table, but he could or would not "direct" them in any way. He manifested a stage of play organization between the autocosmic extension use of toys and their use in the microsphere.

These spheres of representation and dramatization can help us where it is advisable to neglect social connotations, such as what is considered to be a play act, a serious deed, a habit, a symptom, etc., and to find instead in corresponding configurational properties the common denominator for the various parts within the complicated unit of a clinical contact. Our girl patient, for example, manifested the quandary of coöperative retention and elimination on the one side and hateful retention and ejection on the other (plus their relationship to mother and father) in all the three spheres mentioned.

As for the traffic between these spheres of representation we observe that just as an organ, the whole body, a family constellation, or a conception of life as a whole can be represented by a microcosm, so sucking, banging, defecating, etc., when they are prolonged habits, can often be understood as dramatizing social situations and attitudes.

We will readily see that especially for the disturbed child from three to six years old (the age range in our study) autocosmic manifestation leads back easily into the sphere of regressive habits, while macrocosmic expansions make the child try out the environment in a manner both surprising and displeasing to attending adults. There remains then, by force of age preference and expediency, the microsphere as a haven for overhauling the boats before taking further trips into the unknown. Our disturbed children approach this sphere, break down or hesitate before they reach it, experience a disruption in it, or suffer a belated disruption after having over-estimated the omnipotence provided by it. The "sign-magic" used during such behavior seems to us to outline where in the child's life the sphere of relative tolerance borders on the danger sphere of unbearable pressures.

Among such manifestations, that of extrabodily representation of organ-modes, which is the subject of early and special environmental interference, is of outstanding importance for the understanding of preschool play and also for that of all emotionally disturbed older children.

As diagrammatically developed in a previous article (2), the orificial organ-modes incorporation, elimination, retention, and intrusion and the body apertures which are their "models" par excellence, namely mouth, sphincters, and genitals are combined to normal mutual emphasis in successive stages, namely, the stages described by Freud as pre-genital. In each of these stages there is an interrelation between the sensitization and training of a *vital orifice* and the growing *periphery of mastery* (*a*) oral-(respiratory)-sensory-tactual, (*b*) anal-(urethral)-muscular, (*c*) genital-(urethral)-motor. This interrelation can express itself in mode-behavior both *centrifugally as generalization* of the mode, i.e., the mode of the dominant zone becomes the dominant mode of behavior in general, or *centripetally* as a *specialization* of the zone (i.e., a general tendency can express itself in the habits of one zone). For example, the retentive mode may first find emphasis in sphincter-habits and then appear as a general retentive tendency in many aspects of behavior; or it may become noticeable in other habits (such as keeping food in the mouth and neither swallowing nor returning it) and then find its most intensive expression in sphincter-habits. We thus can speak of *mode-fixations* and of *zone-fixations,* the first being a carrying over of one mode from its model-zone to other zones where it is as it were a gesture without functional logic or in the use of one zone for several untimely and displaced modes. Some of these generalizations and specializations are only observable in a limited number of temporarily or permanently fixated children.

"Surveying the field of zone experience and mode manifestation, one finds that what Freud has described as pre-genitality is the development through a succession of narcissistic organ cathexes of impulses and modes of behavior the final integration of which implies all the possible relationships of a body and an object and thus the basic spatial modalities of experience. Led (or confused) by zone experience as well as growing capacity children experiment more or less playfully in space with all the possible relationships of one object to another one and of the body as a whole to space." To modes which in their bodily, spatial, or social expression are curtailed by inhibiting experiences "the organism offers a limited range of safe displacements in habits and minor symptoms. Reality allows for certain systems of subjectified perception; society permits a number of odd social habits and, more or less queer traits. To the child especially the world of play affords opportunity to experiment with organ-modes in extrabodily arrangements which are physiologically safe, socially permissable, physically workable and psychologically satisfying."

Between displacements within the body (habits, symptoms) and the free external displacement in play, we find various arresting combinations. The following example, a previously published (2) non-psychiatric observation, illustrates the way in which the dominance of simple organ-modes during training may for a while govern a child's spheres of behavior. A little boy, *H,* two and one-half years of age, who struggled rather belatedly against enuresis, began to take to bed with him little boxes, which he held closed with both hands. When a box opened during the night, sometimes apparently with his unconscious help, he would cry out in his sleep or awaken and call for someone to help him close it. He would then sleep peacefully, even though not necessarily dry. But he continued to experiment.

During the day he looked around for suitable boxes—obviously driven by an urge to materialize an image of "closedness." Finally he found what seemed to fit the image, a cardboard cylinder which had been the center of a roll of toilet paper. He put two cardboard caps from milk bottles over the openings of the roll. All through the night he would try to hold this arrangement firmly together with both hands—as an animistic guardian of the retentive mode. But no sooner had his training achieved a relative success in closing his body during sleep than he began, *before* going to sleep, to throw all available objects out of the window. When this was made impossible, he stole into other rooms and spilled the contents of boxes and bottles on the floor.

Clearly, the first act, namely holding a closed box as a necessary condition for sleep, resembles a compulsive act originating in the child's fear of failing to retain because of his weakness or because of his wish to expel. Emptying objects, on the other hand, or throwing them out of the window is "delinquent" and the result of the fear of being overpowered by the claims of *society to which he surrenders the zone but not the impulse.* The impulse appears on other levels of representation, where it betrays itself through configurations representing the retentive and eliminative modes.

To prevent the little boy from throwing things out of the window, it was opened from the top. Thereupon he was found riding on it, leaning out into the night. I do not think he would have fallen out; he probably wanted only to show himself "master of openings," as compensation for the surrender of the free use of his excretory openings to society. When, in consequence, his mother kept his window closed until he was asleep, he insisted that the door be left ajar.

Thus not only sections of one's body and toys, but also the body as a whole in its spatial relationship to the whole room or to the whole house, may serve the displaced expression of the impulse in various degrees of compulsive, naughty, or playful acts.

5.

The animal psychologist, having seen rats (whom he had made hungry) learn to run mazes (which he had built) toward food (which he had put there) comes to the conclusion that "the environment takes on for the physiologically aroused organism, by dint of his innate endowment and past experiences, the character of a hierarchy of to-be-sought and to-be-avoided superordinate and subordinate objects" (15).

Essentially, our diagnostic confidence is based on the same expectation, which, however, is derived from the repeated clinical experience that the hierarchy of actually sought-after and avoided toys (offered as stimuli and supports) allow us to draw conclusions in regard to what *has aroused or is arousing the playing organism physiologically and what has happened to it environmentally.* That we cannot consider play an intermission or a vacation from urgent life but rather a continuation of it on a sign level is only our serious adaptation to the serious way in which (given our therapeutic setup) the child behaves with strict selectivity, creates meaningful sign-coherence, and by his emotions betrays a "purpose" where "play" has been suggested.

In describing to the reader, by way of introduction, some of the significant alternatives with which the child is faced on entering the therapeutic situation, and some of the therapist's useful expectancies, we by no means hope to induce him to share what may seem a radical determination. Illustrations can only convince him who already believes that those selected are representative. Therefore I can close this introduction only with the rather inhuman suggestion that a publication like the present one should be read at least twice. Only after the comparison of several cases has made the reader more familiar with the nature of the inventory of possible kinds of behavior from which the individual child makes his choices will he begin to believe that even if presented with different supporting objects the individual child patient could not have produced configurations essentially dissimilar to those which are described in the following pages.

III. STUDIES IN PLAY INTERPRETATION

A. METHOD OF REPRESENTATION

Our material is divided into *contacts* (visits) which in turn consist of *behavior items*. These items are described and discussed in five categories, *A, B, C, D, E,* which indicate the shifting foci of the analytic attention; their peripheries overlap.

A gives a common-sense description of what happens before the observer's eyes; *B* and *C* demonstrate (in slow motion, as it were) two concurrent tendencies in the observers mental activity: *B* is directed toward a future exact description in areas which can also be explored and measured under other than psychiatric conditions; *C* toward the clinicians age-old right and duty to allow himself to be led by subjective factors. The reader should visualize the relationship of *B* and *C*, and their intervention between *A* and *D* in the following manner (Figure 2).

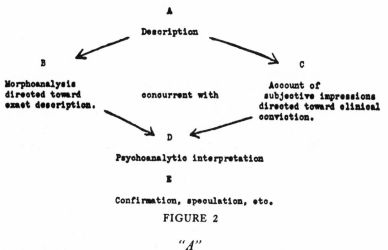

A

Description

B

Morphoanalysis directed toward exact description.

concurrent with

C

Account of subjective impressions directed toward clinical conviction.

D

Psychoanalytic interpretation

E

Confirmation, speculation, etc.

FIGURE 2

"A"

The "behavior item to be analyzed" represents as nearly as possible the span between the moment when we observe that the child has turned his attention to a toy, a person, or a conversational manner, and the moment when we notice that he turns to the next one. This is, of course, a crude concept of an "observational unit"; however, it is the one naturally used in a therapeutic situation in

587

which the task is to infer from the *selective attractions and aversions created by a standard environment* what the patient's relationship may be to certain classes of ideas and thus to discover the pathogenic associations of his mind—which he may keep hidden, which may be unconscious to him, or whose reference and importance may not be understood by him.

"B"

Morphoanalytic description emphasizing the configurations manifested in four areas of behavior:

1.   *Affective:* The patient's manifested emotional *interest in and withdrawal from* the object of the behavior item.

2.   *Ideational:* Verbalized *content,* acted out *themes,* etc.

3.   *Spatial: Configurations* and *modes* in the three spheres of representation.

4.   *Verbal:* Mode of *expression;* speech, voice.

"C"

Observer's Impressions, Associations, and Reflections.   While in *B* the therapist attempts an approximation of objective configurational analysis of what he sees and hears in the currently manifest, in C he *gives impressions* ("it was as if . . .") and *associates past impressions:* previous observation on the child in question or on other children, data communicated to him by the parents, etc.; and he *reflects on latent possibilities,* i.e., the possibility that his associations may correspond to a genetic or associative connection in the child's mind between what he is doing under the observer's eyes and what he is said to have done in other situations.

"D"

Psychoanalytic Interpretation.

1.   His observational and reflective reactions lead the observer to various *interpretational hints.*   A *symbolic equation* or metaphor may make it possible to recognize a play act as alluding to and *standing for an otherwise manifestly avoided* item (person, object, or idea) ; or a *play arrangement* may prove to represent a specific effort on the part of the child to rearrange "in effigy" his psychological position in an experienced or expected danger situation.   Such an arrangement usually corresponds to the child's defense mechanisms (6).

2. If these first hints survive the sifting processes of further observation and investigation, they will sooner or later grow together and create a conviction and an image in the observer's mind in the form of the *reconstruction of a genetic sequence* or of a *dynamic configuration* pertaining to the patient's inner or outer history.

3. The observer may proceed to convey parts of these reconstructions to the child whenever he feels the time has come to do so. This then, is the *therapeutic interpretation.*

"E"

Confirmation of interpretation gained after the contact, and further speculation reaching out beyond the evidence offered by the behavior item.

B. A Six-Year-Old Boy's Secret: John

The observation of the first of our "specimens" led to the discovery of a later verifiable fact, namely, a conscious *secret* kept hidden from the therapist (and his predecessors) by both the child patient and his mother.

John is six years old and a sailor's child. Years of psychiatric investigation have failed to throw light on his impulse to soil himself when overcome by a strange state of rage and sexual excitement. This infantile habit in its importance for the environment has remained the center of a general emotional arrest and of a system of petty delinquency. The mental test shows traces of disintegration and extreme fatigue rather than retardation in his only slightly subnormal intelligence. When he is brought to my attention John is at a hospital where he has undergone (with negative results) an examination of his eliminative organs and an encephalogram; he has also been circumcised. Thus unlike all the other patients to be presented here, John is not brought by his mother. On the contrary (and this is a variation of our model "field situation"), the way back to his mother leads through a successful relationship with me, knowing, as he does, that I will have a word in the final decisions as to his placement, further treatment, etc.

The day before the first regular contact, John had been casually introduced to *Ps*.[13] He had a toy gun in his hand and a dagger at

---

[13]*Ps* == psychoanalyst or psychiatrist, *Pt* == patient.

his side and had exclaimed, *"I am a cop."* When asked, *"Who are you going to shoot?"* he had replied, *"The bad guy."* *"Who is the bad guy?"* *"Me."*

Today *Ps* brings him some plasticine because he was told that John had been sad about the fact that none of the hospital toys were "his own." *Ps* therefore expected John to spend valuable time on the question of which of *Ps*'s toys he would be allowed to take to his room, a common technical problem which can be solved only from case to case and often is of diagnostic value in itself. However, *Ps* did not want to lose any time in this instance and assumed that once the ownership of the play medium was settled *Pt* would concentrate more quickly on whatever he needed to express. *Ps* also considered plasticine to be a fitting "support" for the phantasies of a child who soiled and played with faeces.

1.   *First Contact*

John appears, armed again and looking pale, forlorn, and somewhat scared; he accepts the plasticine with surprised eagerness but without thanks, and immediately concentrates on making an "aeroplane," which, as he says with a shy smile, "brings people from across the ocean." This smile quickly gives way to serious concentration, during which he ignores *Ps* for a while.

"A"

BEHAVIOR ITEM TO BE ANALYZED

Plasticine: Balls

John makes small *balls of plasticine.*
With three blocks he builds *a grocery store.*
"You are the grocery man; I am a truck driver." John fills the truck with the balls and then, elaborately and with a "motor noise" approaches the store, finally dumping the truck's contents into a corner. When asked, "How much does the grocery man owe you," John refuses payment (as if the delivery represented a present to the grocery man). This is repeated.

Suddenly he calls one plasticine ball *mother nut.* Then he takes a smaller ball of the same color and calls it *baby nut.* He then makes of another color plasticine a long row of balls equal in size to the first one and calls them *brother nuts.* **"Whose brothers are they?"** **"My mother's brothers."** You mean uncles?" John becomes very pale, sways as if he were going to faint, and leaves the room hurriedly.

After a while he comes back, obviously from the toilet for he refers to his general state, with the words, "*This is the way I feel when I soil.*" Ps asks once more, "Now tell me, who are your mother's brothers?" John, with a desperate look, "Me."

"*B*"

Morphoanalysis of Manifested Configurations

1. *Affect as manifested in interest and withdrawal:* The interest in the plasticine is first one of hungry *taking* into *possession.* Then follows a short period of quiet *play concentration* out of which suddenly emerges the idea for a *game.* The expression increasingly becomes one of eagerness to play in *coöperation with Ps* and to play *at giving him something.* At the height of this contact-seeking the phantasy of the nut family appears. Some implication of this phantasy then brings about a sudden and vehement play disruption: an anxiety attack and the symptom of sudden defecation make an end to play and game. (What is the dangerous implication of the nut family phantasy?)

2. *Ideational content:* (*a*) Balls are being made; (*b*) groceries are delivered without pay; (*c*) a nut family is represented which consists of a mother, a baby, and many "brothers." (What relation is there between balls, delivery, and the members of a family?)

3. *Spatial expression:* After having put aside his weapons and prepared the balls, Pt seeks intimate *spatial contact with Ps,* trying to win him for a game in which they concentrate together on the microcosmic elaboration of Pt's phantasies. This game is dominated by the configuration of *delivering and dumping.* After the disruption the autocosmic sphere takes the lead and the patient defecates.

It will be seen that the microcosmic play and the autocosmic symptom have in common the *eliminative mode,* the difference being that the balls are dumped as presents in the context of a general contact seeking, the faeces eliminated in anxiety, followed by a general closing up. (What is to be delivered in friendliness, what retained in anxiety?)

4. *Verbal expression:* (*a*) There is probably more than one meaning in the "nuts" which he delivers, the most obvious

being that the family he has in mind is "nuts"; (b) the "me" the day before manifestly expressed the "turning against himself" of the weapons originally intended for "bad guys." Today it turns my questions in regard to the uncles back to him. (Bad uncles in a crazy family? Who are they?)

"C"

IMPRESSIONS, ASSOCIATIONS, REFLECTIONS

John, apparently too starved for gifts to smile or express thanks, accepts the plasticine the way a hungry man reaches for food. (This "aeroplane bringing people from across the ocean" could be equally well associated with either John's absent sailor father or Ps whose accent indicated he had come from far away. Is this the beginning of a transference, i.e., does this express the need for a father?)

John had been described to Ps as a very friendly, accessible, and even voluble boy who craved for a good contact, especially with men. However, at a certain point he would always close up without any real understanding having been reached. When would he close up in the game with the balls which seemed to mean more and more to him as he proceeded?

He made balls, then seemed very eager to play in coöperation with Ps and to deliver something to him, a mode underscored by the refusal of payment which would naturally belong to the commercial play content. This "delinquent" boy who steals and hides what belongs to others and does not even give his faeces at the requested time wants to deliver something to Ps (a father substitute?).

The nuts turn into a family, a mother, and a baby. Is he homesick? One automatically expects next a father and a brother (to complete approximately the actual family constellation), but John lets about fifteen "brothers" follow who are different in color. The number makes Ps suspicious and he asks who they are. The answer, "mother's brothers" could still mean, for example, the many brothers which he expects his mother to produce now that she has started on that line. To make sure which kind of brothers he means, Ps gives him the term for a mother's real brothers.

The word "uncle" seems to hit him like a blow, causes panic with organic symptoms, including the urge to defecate, and ends the game. "Uncles," of course, is not always a correctly used term, and the "different color" suggests that these uncles may not be real relatives, may be outsiders, strangers—John's father is a sailor and the mother has many nights without a husband.

After the disruption and John's return from the toilet, he had answered *Ps*'s last question with "me"—just as he had done that day before when asked, "Who are you going to shoot?" In other words, when asked about the subject of admitted aggressive tendencies, *Pt* had evaded the issue by putting himself jokingly into the rôle of the "guy" whom he wanted to harm. Today, in a much more serious way, he acts as a victim (internalizes somatically) when asked for the identity of somebody who is characterized as "mother's *many* brothers" who in the play family appear in the *father's place* and cause panic when called *"uncles."* If our reflections point in the right direction, John has been made the victim (and has gone on making himself a victim) of an unbearable secret which he does not dare convey, namely, his mother's infidelity or maybe prostitution.

As to our expectation that in John's handling of the clay we would find expressed something of the retentive-eliminative problem which builds the basis of his main symptom, namely his untimely elimination of faeces: We see him all-giving where he plays in delivering the clay balls, apparently unconsciously "giving away" more than he wanted to. Then he tried to close up—and defecates (just as the little girl above had done when deciding to hold on to the pencils). As for the fact that the patient's eliminative system has become the means of expressing ambivalence, constitutional and historical factors will have to be considered. From the anamnesis one fact suggests itself: John was hard to train and his mother beat him often. When, as we assume, he was a witness to his mother's infidelity, i.e., saw her do "dirty" secret and sexual things herself, it is conceivable that he was overcome by hate against the deceitful *M* out of love for whom he had fought himself in an effort to become clean, asexual, and truthful. However, more important at this moment than any reconstruction is the recognition of the conscious factors which block the access to the *Pt*'s confidence.

"D"

PSYCHOANALYTIC INTERPRETATION

1. *Symbols.* (*a*) The *balls* (dumped in playful coöperation) correspond in *consistency* and *mode of use* to *faeces* (which he

ejects in anxiety and anger). (*b*) The *balls* ("mother nut," "baby nut" on the one side, many "brother nuts" on the other) correspond in their most obvious differentiations, namely *color* and *number* to a traumatic family constellation (mother and baby on the one side, many strangers on the other).

2. *Defensive arrangements*: The two sets of symbols correspond to the two main problems (both eliminative-retentive) of the therapeutic situation: (*a*) to the symptom which is to be removed; namely, the untimely elimination of faeces; (*b*) to the first requirement for its removal, namely, the giving away of the mother's secret, which John has succeeded in keeping isolated from all therapeutic confessions made during previous treatment. That *Ps*, instead of asking embarrassing questions, has brought John a present and plays with him, probably increases the (conscious) feeling in John that to be fair with *Ps* he should verbally deliver the secret and thus make the first step toward a new life in which he would learn to retain his faeces. For various reasons, some of which will be made apparent only by further analysis, the patient first resists the overwhelming need to deliver his secret. His defenses are: (*a*) to use the play support offered by *Ps* for the substitution of the delivery of the secret with a delivery in a game. This defense fails when the patient's conversation unconsciously gives away a hint by delivering the strange nut family. (*b*) Noticing this, he uses his second and usual defense; he closes up, as far as the secret behind the hint is concerned, while the eliminative urge expresses itself at its original zone, the eliminative organs. As this happens the conflict between the eliminative and retentive modes and his masochistic tendency to express aroused emotions in a regressive, autocosmic, and punishment-provoking way get the better of him.

3. At the end of this first contact, *Ps* makes only an intentionally vague statement to *Pt*, for which the latter thanks him with a smile. More cannot be done, since it remains necessary to disclose what may be proven to be fact in these "communications," in this case a too delicate investigation with which to burden a child. If the information proves correct, the mother has to be urged to give John permission to talk about *all* his experiences, including those involving her. Only then can we decide how "deep" we have to go to locate the possible damage to John's inner defenses.

"E"

CONFIRMATION AND FURTHER SPECULATION

During *Ps*'s next conversation with the patient's mother, she confessed that there were certain episodes she had urged John not to tell the doctors about, and had added, "Daddy surely would kill me if he heard about it." She asked for psychological help for herself and released John from the promise of secrecy which had blocked previous therapeutic efforts.

The following rudely clinical excerpts from a previous publication (2) may serve to characterize John's further treatment.

"The first barrier which psychoanalysis was forced to attack was the castration fear, which, after the *circumcision, had suppressed his soiling without sublimating the impulse.* Expecting new physical deprivations, the boy would continue to appear equipped with two pairs of eyeglasses on his nose, three knives on a chain hanging out of his trousers and a half dozen pencils sticking out of his vest pocket. Alternately he was a "bad guy" or a cross policeman. He would settle down to quiet play only for a few moments, during which he would choose *little objects* (houses, trees and people) no larger than two or three inches high, and make *covers* for them out of *red plasticine.* But again and again he would become very pale and ask for permission to go to the bathroom.

In describing an automobile accident he had witnessed, in which the chief damage was a *flat tire,* John almost fainted. He felt equally sick when I asked him about certain sleeping arrangements. It appeared that he had seen (in crowded quarters) a man perform intercourse with a woman who sat on him, and he had observed that the man's *penis looked shorter* afterwards. His interpretation of this had been entirely *anal.* Maybe the woman, whose face seemed flushed, had defecated into the man's umbilicus and had done some harm to his genitals. Or the man had, as it were, eliminated a part of his penis into the woman's rectum out of which she later would deliver, i.e., again eliminate, the baby. In addition to the *enlightenment* given that semen and not a part of the penis remained in the woman, the circumcision was talked over and reassurances given for the more important remainder of his genitals.

His first concentrated skilful and sustained play was the following: A caterpillar tractor slowly approached the rear end of a truck, the door of which had been opened. A dog had been placed on the tractor's chain wheels in such a way that he was hurled into the truck at the moment the tractor bumped into it. Obviously he wanted to make sure by *experimenting* with his toys that the pleasant idea of something being thrown into another body without hurting either the giver or the receiver was sensible and workable, although his unresolved anal fixation (no doubt in coöperation with certain common "animalistic" tendencies and observations) did not allow him to conceive of intrusion in any other way than from behind. But it was not as before brown stuff or mud which was thrown, it was *something living* (semen).

Outside the play hours, the eliminative impulse made its reappearance in John's life in macrocosmic fashion. The whole house, the whole body, the whole world was used for the representation of an impulse which did not yet dare to return to its zone of origin. In his sleep, he would start to throw the belongings of other people, and only theirs, out of the window. Then, in the daytime, he threw stones into neighbors' houses and mud against passing cars. Soon he deposited faeces, well wrapped, on the porch of a hated woman neighbor. When these acts were punished, he turned violently against himself. For days he would run away, coming back covered with dirt, oblivious of time and space. He still did not soil, but desperation and the need for elimination became so all powerful that he seemed to *eliminate himself* by wild walks without any goal, coming back so covered with mud that it was clear he must have undressed and rolled in it. Another time he rolled in poison ivy and became covered with the rash.

When he noticed that, by a slowly narrowing network of interpretations, I wanted to put into words those of his impulses which he feared most; namely, elimination and intrusion in their relationship to his mother, he grew pale and resistive. He began a four-day period of faecal *retention,* stopped talking and playing, and stole excessively, hiding the objects. As all patients do, he felt rightly that verbalization means detachment and resignation: He did not dare to do the manifest, but he did not want to give up the latent.

He did not live at home at this time. After many weeks, he received the first letter from his mother. Retiring to his room, he shrank, as it were, physically and mentally, and soiled himself. For a while he did this regularly whenever his mother communicated with him. It was then possible to interpret to him his ambivalent love for his mother, the problems of his bowel training, and his theories concerning his parents' bodies. It was here also that his first free *flow of memories* and associations appeared, allowing us to verbalize much that had been dangerous only because it had been amorphus.

One day he suddenly expressed the wish to make a poem. If there ever was a child who, in his make-up and behavior, did not lead one to expect an aesthetic impulse, it was John. Nevertheless, in a *flood of words,* he now began to dictate song after song about beautiful things. Then he proposed the idea, which he almost shrieked, of sending these poems to his mother. The act of producing and writing these poems, of putting them into envelopes and into the mailbox, fascinated him for weeks. He *gave something to his mother* and it was *beautiful!* The intense emotional interest in this new medium of expression and the general change in habits accompanying it, indicate that by means of this act of sending something beautiful to his mother the eliminative impulse had found a higher level of expression: the zone submitted to training."

C. A Neurotic Episode in a Girl of Three

The second case should bridge to some extent the short and all too "obvious" first and the longer and very complex third examples. Among the writer's Boston notes, he finds the following encounter with a charming but badly scared little girl who was friendly enough to provide a basis for diagnosis in *two contacts.* We shall call her Mary.

The complaint was that shortly before her third birthday Mary had developed nightmares during which she struck about wildly; at about the same time, after a dozen visits to a play group organized by a group of mothers in a suburb, she had been overcome by violent anxiety attacks with uncontrollable crying. An attempt had been made to let Mary's mother stay in or near the nursery, but this arrangement had helped only temporarily. The routine situations of afternoon rest and going to the toilet seemed provocative factors in the outbreaks of anxiety.

It must be noted however, that Mary had no attacks during her first visits to the play group, although she showed some tenseness and some rigidity of posture and behavior. When the attacks began, the play group leader as well as the mother felt that something in the nursery must have frightened her. We shall concentrate on the way this complicated something was revealed during the first two contacts with me.

1. *First Contact*

Mary, dark-haired, attractive, is slight but well built. Her walk is somewhat stiff and her handshake rigid, but she seems well coördinated.

"*A*"

Mother

Holds mother's hand as she enters office. When she shakes hands with *Ps*, she gives him a brief smile, then immediately turns her head away and from then on tries not to look at him. She turns to her mother, puts arms around her, and keeps her near the open door. While *M* tries to encourage her to look at the toys, she closes her eyes tightly, hides her face in *M*'s skirt, repeats in a babyish voice, "*Mommy, mommy, mommy.*"

"*B*"

I

1. After a short glance into the room and a very short and slightly coquettish contacting of *Ps* in whom *M* tries to interest her, Mary withdraws to her mother.

2. Spatially keeping near the open door, she clings babyishly to *M*'s body (adherence) as if she wanted to hide in it, and excludes *Ps* to the extent of closing her eyes very tightly so as not to see him (encasement). No selectiveness in regard to the toys is evident.

"*C*"

I

She first looks at me as if she wanted to see whether or not the new adult is going to understand fun. However, this feeler is quickly withdrawn; her flight to her mother seems somewhat dramatic. I am not sure that she is not hiding a smile. It seems that she did not show any similar reaction to either the secretary or to a lady who spoke to her in the waiting room; the first impression is that she is conscious of my being a man (doctor) and that there is a coquettish element in her behavior.

"*A*"

II

MOTHER AND DOLL

Pointing to a (girl) doll, Mary asks *M* several times, "What that, what that?" After *M* has explained that it is a dolly, Mary repeats in a babyish way, "*Dolly, dolly, dolly,*" and suggests in words not understandable to *Ps* that *M* take off the dolly's shoes. *M* tries to induce her to perform this act herself, but Mary simply repeats her demands again and again without listening to *M*.

"*B*"

II

1. Her interest in the doll is not able to overcome her reluctance to play; she *makes her mother play.*
2. The content: Mother dresses, undresses a *girl* doll's *feet.*
3. Thus Mary draws the doll into the mother adherence.
4. Her speech remains babyish, repetitious.

"*A*"

III

INTERRUPTION

M begins to feel embarassed since the hour is assuming the character of an observation of her in her play with Mary. She asks, therefore, if it is not time for her to leave the room and to wait outside. *Ps* approves of her decision. Mary does not show any signs of fear when, the adherence to *M* being thus broken up, she suddenly finds herself without anybody to lean on.

"*C*"

III

Mary showed the same initial lack of anxiety when left by *M* in the nursery school. It seems that either something specific must happen to provoke manifest anxiety or that her anxiety typically remains latent for a while.

"A"

IV

Doll

M has left the doll in Mary's hand. Mary grasps it firmly around its legs. Suddenly she smiles mischievously, her face flushes, and she begins to touch various things in the room with the doll's head. When a toy falls from the shelf, she laughs and begins to push smaller toys, always with the doll's head, in such a way that they fall too. Her excitement increases, manifested by chuckling and laughter. With special glee she pushes (with the doll's head) a toy train which is on the floor in the middle of the room. As one car overturns, she overturns them all. But then she suddenly stops and becomes very pale.

She leans with her back against the sofa, holds the doll over her genital region and drops it on the floor. She picks it up again, holds it over the same region, and drops it again. While repeating this from ten to fifteen times, she begins first to whine, then to cry, finally to yell, *"Mommy, mommy, mommy."*

(*M*, sure that the game is up, enters room to take Mary home.)

"B"

IV

1. The sudden hilarity and blushing aggressiveness immediately enters into a dramatic curve of quickly increasing excitement. This likewise suddenly reverts to pale inhibition and overt anxiety. Her blind screaming contacts her mother and restores the mother adherence.

2. The discernible content has been: *Pushing and throwing down* of things, not with her hand but with an extension of her hand; the *dropping* from the genital region of a doll (which before, as an extension of the hand, had been, as it were, a pushing tool).

3. Spatially, after the physical adherence to *M* is made impossible, the child turns in a diffused way to the room at large and to the small toys in it. Her play is of the *autocosmic extension* type with the doll used as an extension of the pushing hand. Only in pushing the train does she approach a possible *microcosmic theme* (train accident); where-

upon she withdraws to the periphery of the room where she dramatizes the loss from the genital region of the doll which had been an extension of the aggressive hand. Paralyzed by anxiety, she then contacts her mother who leads her out of the conflict situation.

4. Corresponding to this aggressive and regressive behavior, her loud communication changes from coquettish chuckling to excited laughter, to pale silence, to anxious whining, to desperate screaming, "*Mommy. mommy, mommy.*"

"*C*"

IV

The doll in Mary's hand is used in such a way as to appear that she does not dare touch or push the objects with her bare hand. One is reminded that in the play group her strange way of touching and lifting things ("never with the whole hand") was observed. This and a certain rigidity in the extremities suggest that Mary is (constitutionally or traumatically) disturbed in the manipulative and locomotor sphere.

The way in which she then seems unable to stop her own dramatization of something dropping from the genital region reminds one of the interpretation given to certain hysterical (grand mal) attacks in which the patient is supposed to represent both partners in an imagined scene, namely, the victim and the aggressor in a sexual act. Here it would be the robbed and the robber. Literally, the dropping of a doll from between the legs suggests "birth." The half-sitting position she assumes when dropping the doll suggests a "toilet situation." Birth and toilet situation have in common the "dropping" of (valuable) bodily content. While we know nothing about the events of Mary's toilet training period, it seems that in the nursery the toilet situations were factors in the outbreak of her anxiety. Finally the association with "extension" (and pushing?) suggests that she may be dramatizing the fact that she has no penis. It is most probable that on entering the nursery school Mary was given her first opportunity to go to the toilet in the presence of boys and to see boys' genitals. Is this the "loss" which she indicates?

"*D*"

IV

1. Symbols: The doll, first a baby (with shoes), is then used as (*a*) a hand extension (finger?); (*b*) a genital extension (penis or bodily content?).

Of defensive arrangements the following were recognizable: at the beginning and at the end of the hour self-protection by means of regressive *M*-adherence and denial of interest in toys and *Ps*; during the pushing episode, protection of extremity by the use of an (overcompensatory?) extension. The defense arrangement breaks down as Mary is overcome by the impulse to push and by some phantasy of the loss of the extension. We may therefore say:

2. Mary seems to be full of mischief (so far expressed as aggressive pushing), but is afraid of her impulses because she may damage her hand or lose something in the genital region if she does not restrict her sphere of expression and keep close to her mother.

3. The contact offered neither the opportunity nor the appropriate moment for the administration of a therapeutic interpretation. If the mother had not interrupted (a behavior which throws some light on her part in the child's anxiety situations) *Ps* would have tried to get in some kind of verbal contact with the child.

2. *Interview with Mother*

In a conversation with *M* the child's total situation at the time of her visits to the nursery is discussed. *M* relates a fact which she had forgotten to tell me before: Mary had been *born with a sixth finger* which had been removed when she was approximately a half-a-year old. Just prior to the outbreak in the play group Mary had frequently asked about the *scar* on her hand and had received the answer that it was "just a mosquito bite." The mother admits, however, that the child in somewhat younger years could easily have been present when her operation was discussed. Around the time of her anxiety Mary had been equally insistent in her *sexual curiosity*, a fact which speaks for the possible importance at that time of a "scar" association between the actually lost finger and the mythical lost penis.

Her curiosity had received a severe blow when, shortly before the outbreak of anxiety, her father, irritable because of an impending legislative decision, had *shown impatience with her during her usual morning visit* to him in the bathroom and had shoved her out of the room. She had liked to watch the shaving process and had also frequently on recent occasions (to his annoyance) asked about his genitals. It must be taken into account here that a strict adherence to a certain routine situation in which she could do, say, and ask the same thing over and over again always had been a necessary condition for Mary's inner security.

As to the child's physical condition at these particular times, it appears that bad dreams with violent kicking in sleep (which M tries to check by holding her tight and awakening her), and foul breath on awakening had been attributed by one physician to a *bad condition of the tonsils*. Another physician, however, had denied this. The mother and the first physician had engaged in a heated discussion (before Mary) as to whether she needed an immediate *operation*. Before we evaluate all these factors (which add the association "operation" to that of "scar" and explain both an increased adherence to M during F's irritable absent-mindedness and an increased fear of doctor-possibilities), we shall report Mary's second contact in order to see which of all these factors her further play will single out as subjectively relevant.

"A"

I

MOTHER

Mary again smiles bashfully at me, again turns her head away, holding on to M's hand and insisting that M come with her into the room. Once in the room, however, she lets her mother's hand go and as M and Ps sit down she begins to play peacefully and with concentration.

"A"

II

BUILDING A HOUSE WITH BLOCKS

Mary goes to the corner where the blocks are on the floor. She selects two blocks and arranges them in such a way that she can stand on them each time she comes to the corner to pick up the other blocks. She carries the blocks to the middle of the room, where she has put a toy cow, and builds a very small house. For about 15 minutes she is completely absorbed in the task of arranging the house so that it is strictly rectangular and at the same time fits tightly about the cow. She then adds several blocks to the long side of the house in the following way (Figure 3).

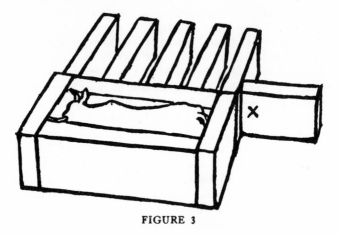

FIGURE 3

At the point marked X she adds a sixth extension, shifting it several times to other places, but finally returning it definitely to X.

"B"

II

1. Today Mary peacefully concentrates on microcosmic play with a certain maternal quality of care and order. There is no climax of excitement, and the play ends on a note of satiation.

2. Her play has as subject (a) the building of a close-fitting stable for a toy cow; (b) adorning the stable building with six wings (five plus one).

3. Though M is present, Mary does not seem moved by impulses of adherence. She builds freely in the middle of the room, moving to the corner and back without hesitation.

Play again begins with an autocosmic extension, namely creating a base for the feet, and then is microcosmic throughout. The block configuration suggests, first, the female protective mode; second, a hand with a sixth finger or a foot with a sixth toe.

"C"

II

The mother has remained in the room, not "good technique," but before this can be changed, Mary has concentrated so deeply on her play that it seems better to let her finish it.

Mary, with all her rigidity, balances well standing on the two blocks and bending down. The fact that she has to create a foot extension (protection? overcompensation?) for herself before picking up blocks reminds us of the fact that during the previous contact she had to add an extension (the doll) to her hand before she pushed the objects in the room. Both these acts suggest, of course, the association: scar, operation.

The house is built with a special expression of maternal "care." The five wings, to which (after some doubt as to where to put it) a sixth is added, again remind one of the amputation of her sixth finger.

But this time, although again beginning with the representation of the extension of an extremity, Mary's play does not lead into an aggressive outbreak (and the subsequent representation of a catastrophe). It finds satiation in the building of a female protective configuration. There is a pervading femininity about today's behavior which serves to underscore in retrospect and by contrast the danger dramatized during the first contact, namely, the loss from the genital region of an object used for aggressive pushing. The interesting combination of a handlike configuration with one which we are used to interpret as symbolizing the female organs of procreation furthermore suggests that a masturbation threat (harm to hand or genital if in contact) may be one of the specific experiences to which the little girl is reacting with anxiety.

"D"

II

1. *Symbols.* (a) blocks—protection—extension of feet—; (b) blocks—building—female protective configuration around

animal—safe body content; (c) blocks—extensions of building
—six fingers to a hand.

2. *Defensive arrangement.* Maternal herself and master
of the microsphere, Mary restores her body's inviolability by
representing as restituted the losses alluded to during the first
contact: her feet are extended (protected?); the content of
her female body (baby) is well protected; the sixth finger
is returned to the hand. The play ends on a note of satiety.

"A"

III

GAME WITH Ps

Suddenly Mary looks teasingly at Ps, laughs, takes M's
hand and pulls her out of the room, saying, "Mommy, come out."

Ps waits for a while then looks out into the waiting room.
He is greeted with a loud and triumphant "Thtay in there!"
Ps withdraws, whereupon Mary closes the door with a bang.
Two further attempts on the part of Ps to leave his room
are greeted in the same way.

(After a while, Ps opens the door slightly, quickly pushes
the toy cow into the other room, makes it squeak and withdraws it again. Mary is beside herself with pleasure and
insists that the game be repeated again and again until,
finally, it is time for her to go home.

When she leaves she looks at Ps directly, shakes hands in
a natural way, and promises to "come back").

"B"

III

1. After being satiated with peaceful building, Mary suddenly and teasingly turns to me to initiate a game. During
the game it is noticeable that, in spite of her aggressive
hilarity, she does not tend (as she did during the first contact) toward overdoing aggressiveness and then withdrawing
from it; Mary is in the real spirit of the game up to the
time she has to leave.

2. The game has as content: A man (Ps) is teasingly
locked into his room alone.

3. This game is macrocosmic indeed. Mary is the
master, not only of both the waiting room and my office (and

the connecting door), but also of her mother and especially of me. She takes M out of my space and locks me into it.

4. "Thtay in there" are the *first words* she has ever addressed to me. They are said clearly and in a loud voice.

"C"

III

Mary's provocative behavior came very suddenly and with determination, as if something in her had waited for the moment when she would be free enough to initiate this game. What does it mean? The day before I had asked the mother to leave the room in the middle of the hour. Has Mary anticipated the repetition of this, and has she arranged her triumphant going out of the room with M in place of my sending M out without Mary? The situation does not seem covered by this possible interpretation.

The words which Mary uses when initiating the game somehow resemble the words which the mother told me the father had used when locking the child out of the bathroom during his days of irritation. *"Stay out of here,"* had been the father's angry words. *"Thtay in there"* is probably linked with it, although in addition to the transference to me a double reversal has taken place: from the passive to active (it is she who gives orders), and in regard to the vector (she "encloses" instead of being excluded). One remembers now that from the moment Mary came into my room at the beginning of the first contact she showed a somewhat coquettish and bashful interest in me. Since it can be expected that she would transfer to me (the man with the toys) a conflict which disturbed her usually playful relationship to her father, it seems possible that in this game she is repeating with active mastery ("You thtay in there") the situation of exclusion of which she has been a passive victim at home ("Stay out of here"). (This possibility came to me only after I had reacted to her play provocation, which, of course, I was prepared to do as soon as she would have chosen the moment and the theme. By my play acts I unconsciously took the rôle of the "good father" in a specific, symbolic way.)

"D"

III

1. *Arrangement.* After having assumed the good mother rôle (mother identification) and having protected and restored

her body (restitution), Mary is transferring to me the rôle of the bad father (father transference) in a rearrangement of the situation which created the conflict between them (reversal of active into passive).

2. We do not know why the second contact was peaceful. It often happens that once excessively fearful doctor-expectations are disproved (they are, of course, more easily disproved in less neurotic children), the problems which had been previously presented in all their horrors appear in the form of restitutions: peaceful and playful identification with her mother, protection and restitution of her body in play, and the teasingly revengeful restitution of the play relationship to her father in transference. The child, as it stands at the end of the second contact, has indicated that she wants to be sure of her mother as a haven of protection, of her father as an interesting masculine playmate, and of her body as an inviolable whole in spite of the (at the time intrusive) impulses it expresses and the bodily dangers (operation) experienced and anticipated.

"E"

III

After a play contact which gave the therapist some first insight and the patient some long needed partial play satisfaction, there remain the following therapeutic questions: how normal for her age are the child patient's problems, how much essential stability and adaptability has she betrayed, and how much support can she expect from her environment.

4. *Etiological Speculations*

We may now inquire into the factors in Mary's life to which our attention has been drawn by her play. Now, as at any deeper point of clinical investigation, we seek to gain insight into changes in the following three segments of the patient's life and into their particular functional relation; namely, into the *coincidence in time* and the *mutual aggravation* of (a) changes in the *physiological sphere* as they are brought about by decisive epigenetic steps in *growth and maturation,* or by some special disbalancing factor such as *sickness or accident;* (b) changes in the constellation or the emotional temperature in the *environment;* (c) changes in the person's *conception of his status* in the world, i.e., a subjectivation of causal judgment in terms of guilt, inferiority, projected intentions, etc.

We find in a disturbed adult's life history that a set of conscious and unconscious ideas (a "complex") is subjectifying his experiences, making all changes mutually aggravating, bringing about continuous libidinal disequilibrium and making the individual the easy "traumatic" victim of specific types of occurrences. Usually the "complex" dates far back—and, indeed, we can observe in still undisturbed children that it is one or the other normal maturational crisis, with its complex of wishful and fearful expectations, during which (given a certain lack of psychosomatic or social support) experiences of a specific type or combination become traumatic: perception is subjectified, anxiety increases, defensiveness stiffens.

Once the mechanisms of psychological homeostasis have been upset for a long time and the individual finally is forced to seek help from a representative of a healing method, content and morphology of his sickness show such a multiple relation to an endless number of factors seemingly making one another pathogenic that unlimited material is provided for the discussion of whether the condition has a physiological or psychological basis. Usually, reality forces a simple solution: whatever method by right or might can claim the patient, is able to secure a selection of data and, by interjecting its curative agent, is successful in breaking the vicious circle of pathogenic factors will also determine the only "evidence" of the circle's "beginning" which anybody will ever have.

We hope to approach such problems from a new angle through the study in normal or only temporarily disturbed children of those periods of lowered physiological resistance, those types of lowered environmental support, and those mechanisms of attempts at adjustment which, if occurring together, represent a combination producing traumatic strain.

Mary's disclosure of her personality in her present stage of maturation and state of anxiety, shows her generally somewhat *timid*: in all her aggressiveness she likes to have the retreat to her mother well covered. She is *rigid* in the sense that changes of routine are in themselves upsetting. On the other hand she is playfully *mischievous* and psychosexually *girlish*. There is no doubt that Mary is *dramatic* (an interesting hysterical contrast to some of her compulsive traits) lovable, playful, outgoing, coquettish if master of the situation; stubborn, babyish, and shut-in when disturbed.

Physiological changes: maturational. Mary's age and play suggest that she may be considered to be in the stage of childhood characterized (in both sexes) by a rapidly increasing power of *locomobility,* expanding *curiosity,* and *genital sensuality,* which in psychoanalytic literature is called the phallic stage and for which the author, in order to take into account certain developmental facts, has used the terms locomotor-phallic or "intrusive stage" (3).

The intrusive stage, in analogy to other stages, emphasizes sometimes silently, sometimes more noisily the following developmental potentialities:

1. The *impulse* of intrusion (epigenetically emerging with added vigor from the inventory of given impulses), the urge to force one's way into the object of interest and passion.

2. The *sensual* (*libidinal*) *experiences* of increased locomotor pleasure and (often masturbatory) indulgence in phantasies of intrusive conquest.

3. A channel for the *release* (catharsis) of *surplus tension* from various sources in relatively excessive activity, of an aggressive, curious, and masturbatory character.

4. Specific trial and error *experiments* in regard to how far one can go in physically and socially forcing one's way into the sphere of others.

5. A complex of *omnipotence and impotence phantasies* depicting the child either in the unlimited execution of the intrusive mode, and the unlimited mastery over its phantasy object (omniscient master of the universe, conquering the mysterious, taking revenge on giant enemies, etc.) or as the victim of other masters.

6. A new focus for the expectation of danger (*developmental fear*), i.e., an intolerance toward all interferences which may bring frustration to 1, 2, and 3, and danger to the organs involved. If increased by constitutional or environmental factors this intolerance may lead to an abnormal intensity or prolongation of 3 (i.e., excessive aggressiveness or masturbation) and severe anxiety and rage in the face of attempts to break it.

7. *Reaction* formations, i.e., changes in the personality which can be understood as permanent defensive reactions of the ego against those aspects of 1-5 which can neither be quite outgrown nor successfully used in socially approved action patterns.

To the future of the personality this stage (like all the others) provides a source of experiential wealth and power as well as of danger.

8. The personality is strengthened and enriched by (a) the successfully socialized use (sublimation) of the new impulse for such growing abilities and aspirations as are in accord with ego and environment: outgoingness and energy, courage in the face of the unknown, etc.; (b) by reliable *reactive* virtues binding some of the excessive energy and the unsuitable modes of the stage, such as self-restraint, protective attitudes, etc.

9. The danger consists in the potential *developmental fixation* which may build the basis for a future (periodic or permanent) *developmental regression,* such as the sadomasochistic dealing with partners in love or work. Reaction formations while creating virtues under certain conditions may imply excessive and permanent inhibition of intrusive types of action, repression of corresponding thoughts and past experiences or more radical measures such as the "turning against oneself" of intrusive acts and thoughts, i.e., masochistic fantasies, often with organic concomitants, or with the provocation of bad treatment by others.

In every developmental stage there is a period when a momentary fixation threatens to become incompatible with progression—the most common kernel of neurotic episodes in childhood. Such neurotic episodes are, of course, similar in content and form to the manifestations of chronic neurotics.

The study of neuroses has shown us that special educational interferences with the general mode of the intrusive stage (such as Victorian tendencies to place special limitations on many forms of locomotor and curious expansiveness, and to react with disciplinary selectivity to sexual curiosity) result in a fixation on the idea of genital intrusion, making the genitals the subject of excessive cathartic acts or that of excessive curiosity and often the consequently excessive repression of both. Such fixation brings with it a prolonged emphasis on the idea and the fear of intruding and on the idea and fear of being intruded upon and, consequently, fears for the inside of the body (as a goal of intrusion) and for extremities and penis as the organs of intrusive aggressiveness. Such a body of fearful expectations becomes, then, a ready factor in the traumatic nature of corresponding experiences.

It must be obvious that this stage offers special problems to the girl. Led by the intersexual experiences of younger organisms, she too has reached a period of stronger intrusive tendencies, often observed as tomboyishness. During this period clitoral masturbation and phantasies of having or achieving a penis (with all the locomotor and mental prerogatives ascribed to it) are not infrequently admitted. We know that in certain types and under certain cultural conditions this wish remains dangerously determining for life, while often, in a way much less well known, the locomotor-phallic complex seems easily and, so to speak, noiselessly subordinated to the wish for a baby and all the prerogatives connected with *this* possibility. But the physiological and psychological conditions which the girl must accept while imagining for the first time becoming the object of intrusive impulses and developing and libidinizing the (not necessarily unaggressive or passive) impulses of inception, make the problem of female masochism a cardinal one—for personality as well as for culture. Of the mature man and the mature woman we expect that both the sadistic and the masochistic aspects of sexual intrusion have been subordinated to a satisfactory mutuality. This ideal of sexual maturity presupposes the successful liquidation of the phantasies and fears of the intrusive stage, during which to the bewildered child "cruel" and "sexual" often seem synonyms (3).

Mary, as little as she told us so far, has revealed something of the conflict of the girl who does not know whether she wants to be a boy or a boy's girl—although she has done so with more grace and humor than we could expect from the chronic victims of this conflict.

We also understand that during her first contact Mary indicated to us that she had associated the intrusive impulses of the stage just outlined with the idea of *"danger to the extremities"*—an association probably preconsciously emphasized by the allusions to her *lost finger* and the imminent danger of an *operation*. However, during her second contact she dramatizes the development of a female identification and mastery of the fears of the intrusive stage.

In regard to the necessary attachment to one or both of her parents of these impulses and fears ("Oedipus Complex") we can only say that the therapist in this case naturally attracted the father-transference; there seems to be little doubt as to the importance at this time of the child's father as a partner in teasing games and as an object of sexual curiosity. The child's flight to her mother is by no means free of ambivalence, as further observation would quickly reveal.

Physiological changes: special physiological condition. Mary has not been sleeping well of late. She has severe panics (or tantrums) in her sleep, during which she yells, *"No, no, no!"* Whatever it may be that she is dreaming about, she awakens with a foul breath and there is a suspicion that the state of her *throat* causes irritation and contraction even if there is no indication for a tonsillectomy. She has heard of the possibility of an operation which she seems to have associated with the loss of her finger.

Environmental changes. The sudden addition to her sphere of experience of the *play group* puts Mary for the first time in her life in the hands of an adult other than a near relative and into a play situation with boys (at home there is only an older sister). Both her *maturational* state and the *idea of an operation* as associated with the loss of the finger must give the observation of sexual differences (in children) at this moment, even if it has been observed before, a sudden specific pathogenic importance.

At *home* it seems to be the *father's irritability* which the child, not knowing the cause, must have misunderstood and connected with the place where it was first experienced (or because of obvious associations most intensely experienced); namely, the *bathroom.* Thus this experience, too, has been incorporated into the field of *mutually specific factors.*

We shall now offer a tentative diagrammatical summary, (*a*) comprising the interrelation of the historical, maturational, special physiological, and environmental changes, with the impulses, ideas, and fears which we suspect of forming parts of the anxiety content; and (*b*) leading us back to the behavior items which "told us" of these impulses, ideas, and fears (Table 1).

What I have said about Mary, represents the "mental note" which the psychoanalyst would make tentatively at the end of the two contacts. Some parts of the note would stand out in more clarity than others; however, we would expect him to have the courage to modify even his "clear impressions" if further observations demanded it.

As for Mary, the contacts were interrupted by a vacation period after which the observer left Boston. Therefore Mary's situation was carefully discussed with her understanding parents who ac-

TABLE 1
DIAGRAMMATIC SUMMARY

The diagonal (*A-G*) shows the historical, maturational, and environmental changes which seem to be of acute importance in the patient's present life situation. Downward and to the left of the diagonal (*AB-FG*) the possibly and probably resulting emotional emphases are shown. Emphasis *AB* is the result of the mutual aggravation of change *A* and *B*: *AC* that of *A* and *C*; etc. Upwards and to the right of the diagonal (*ab-fg*) the play acts are shown which made us aware of the actuality and motivating power of the ideas and emotions shown in *AB-FG*: *ab* points to *AB*, *ac* to *AC*, etc. However, play acts are "overdetermined", i.e., correspond to several ideas and emotions.

	A	B	C	D	E	F	G
A	**A** HISTORICAL: amputated finger	*ab* autosphere: hysterical dramatization: loss from genital region protective overcompensation: microsphere: extensions of hand and foot restoration: female protective configuration and six-finger configuration					
B	**AB** 1. fear for (aggressive) extremities. 2. masochistic fantasies?	**B** MATURATIONAL I intrusive (phallic) vs. female protective impulses	*bc* defense: bashfulness before play expression: exhibitionistic elements in hysterical dramatization transference: provocative mischievousness in play with P_1	*bd* defense: hysterical elements in play dramatization	*be, ce, de* mixture of coquetry (man) and fear (doctor)	*bf, cf* defense: mother adherence and shying away from toys	*bg, cg* symptom: anxiety attacks in nursery
C	**AC** association scar-vagina	**BC** sexual curiosity and feeling of shame	**C** MATURATIONAL II curiosity vs. bashfulness	*cd* transference and sublimation: curiosity in regard to P_1's train (page 615)			
D	**AD** theory that mother evades the scar-vagina issue because she caused these losses?	**BD** Provocative mischievousness in play with father,	**CD** curiosity in regard to father's body	**D** MATURATIONAL III need for (and fear of) father; need for (and jealousy of) mother "ambivalence"		*df, ef* transference in mastersymbolic play: transformation of "doctor"-situation into "playing with man"-situation and "rejection" of P_1 (reversal); *symptom:* play disruption with new mother adherence	*dg, eg* regression: babyish mother adherence
E	**AE** association: amputation of finger—loss of penis—operation on tonsils	**BE** general fear of being intruded upon	**CE** fear of physical examinations	**DE** fear dreams ("no, no!")	**E** PHYSIOLOGICAL throat condition (threatened operation)		
F	**AF** theory of chirurgical punishment	**BF** guilt feelings for mischievousness	**CF** guilt feelings for curiosity	**DF** feeling of being rejected by father	**EF** feeling of impending danger	**F** ENVIRONMENTAL I father's temporary irritability	*fg* see dg
G	**AG** feeling of having been robbed of important organs	**BG** mischievous intentions and anticipating fears in contacts with boys?	**CG** curiosity in regard to children's genitals	**DG** need for mother	**EG** feeling of danger	**FG** devaluation of "big girl"-hood; need for mother	**G** ENVIRONMENTAL III new play group (with boys)

cepted (and partly themselves suggested) the following recommendations. Mary's curiosity in regard to both her scar and her genitals required a truthful attitude. She needed to have other children and especially boys visit her for play at her home. The matter of the tonsils called for the decision of a specialist which could then be candidly communicated to the child. It did not seem wise to awaken and hold her during her nightmares; perhaps she needed to fight her dreams out, and there would be opportunity to comfort her when she awoke spontaneously. The child needed much locomotor activity; playful instruction in rhythmic movements might help her to overcome some rigidity in her extremities which, whatever the cause, presumably has been increased since she heard for the first time about the amputation of her finger.

A conversation with the parents a half year after the contacts described in this report did not seem to indicate the immediate necessity for further psychoanalytic observation. A tonsillectomy had proved unnecessary; the nightmares had ceased; Mary was making free and extensive use of the new play companions provided in and near her home. For various circumstantial reasons, she had, however, not visited the original play group again. She had asked for *Ps* often, wanting to know the color of the train he had taken when leaving town.

When Mary, a while later, paid *Ps* a short visit, she was entirely at home and asked *Ps* in a clear, loud voice about the color of his train. She addressed *M* and *Ps* alternately and entered *Ps's* room without anxiety. Her play immediately centered around the cow again, which, with loving words, was given a tight-fitting stable.

D. Orality in a Boy of Four

Dick was brought to our attention by a physician from a nearby town who occasionally attended the meetings of our Yale study group. His mother, the physician's patient, had complained for the last year or so of a "queer trait" in her little boy; encouraged by our work, the physician, an extraordinarily good observer, familiar with the principles of psychoanalysis, decided to try her eye on the child's play. She invited the little boy, who had never seen her, to come to her office to play and reported to us the five contacts, the first three of which will be given here.

Dick on his fourth birthday was a physically healthy, attractive, and intelligent child who had a good appetite and slept well. However, he was often dreamy and withdrawn and, with strange indifference, would express rather queer fears and concepts. His parents, warned by outsiders, began to fear that "some day he might withdraw completely and not come out of it." They had had this in mind for some time when suddenly, at four years and two months of age, he calmly refused to speak for 24 hours and for some days after would only whisper. Such "spells" recurred.

It had started during a big family dinner. An uncle's completely bald head fascinated Dick. Innocently, he remarked, *"You haven't any hair on your head."* The adults smiled in embarrassment and hoped he would think of something else, but a few moments later he addressed the bald-headed man again. *"Have you no comb at your house?"* After more such remarks Dick's grandmother took him aside and told him that he was "not to talk about this any more." The child, without any display of emotion, became silent and remained silent for 24 hours, except for some whispered remarks in school the next morning.

Naturally, the parents were worried about such a radical reaction to an everyday occurrence such as the prohibition against talking about a seemingly unimportant matter. On the other hand, it was hard to judge the "seriousness" of Dick's reaction for he seemed neither stubborn, nor worried, nor angry; he simply was far away, apparently uninterested in a means of communication which had proved so troublesome.

One remembered then that on several occasions Dick had been a radical representative of the biblical saying, *"If thine eye offend thee, pluck it out"*—or rather its infantile form, *"If thine eye offend thy parents, pluck it out."* There had been, for example, a time (it was during one of his mother's pregnancies) when he was very proud of and liked to display and brag about his "nice fat tummy." Its unproductivity devaluated the possession of this part of his body, whereupon he remarked that he was going to throw it out of the window and was found pressing it against a hot radiator "to burn it off." Similarly, after one of his little sisters had been born and had taken supremacy in the family's attention, he seemed ready to cast away all the prerogatives of his age and sex. He began to creep, to use baby talk, and even to want his clothes and his belongings to be called "little." Again, he not only tried to deny a devaluated possession, this time his genitals, but was found attempting "to pull them off," and finally asked his distraught parents to do him this service.

It would be hard to say exactly whether and where all this transgresses the range of variations and episodic peculiarities of normal child behavior. To his intimate observers, Dick seemed to *experiment with reality* in a somewhat less playful and more deeply preoccupied way than most children do. He was interested in parts of the body (the "tummy" of a pregnant woman, the penis) which are of outstanding importance in some cases, but are missing in others without apparent disadvantage for either well-being or prestige. This preoccupation with missing things could take possession of him to such a degree that the majority of his remarks and questions during a given period would indicate a concept of the world in which *missing things* were not the exception but the rule and the dominant aspects. After he had been frightened by the sight of eyeglasses, he asked everyone, including perfect strangers, whether their eyes came out. After he had discovered that a certain old man had false teeth, he asked the same question about everybody's teeth. When he saw a sculptured bust, he remarked that it had "no feet"; on entering a room, he pointed to what looked to him like holes in the ceiling before he noticed anything else. To him, a person did not "have" a tummy or an arm, but "wore" them; an expression which clearly implied the suspicion that these parts could be taken off like clothes.

Thus, at times, his body image seemed to lack a certain integrity. But while his calmness suggested that this lack was simply the remnant of an earlier age, i.e., represented a maturational deficiency, his usual display of intelligence contradicted this interpretation. Consequently, it was necessary to assume that the boy experienced (or pretended to experience) rather something of a disintegration of his body image.

An attempt to test Dick's intelligence had the following result:

> In many instances the child appeared to be concentrating on the task at hand. At other times he seemed almost like a sleepwalker. The very much longer time required for the third trial of the Sequin form board may be attributed to the fact that two or three times he simply became fixated on a block and was unable to continue the activity. When a key

was held out to him and he was asked to name it, he seemed
to look right through it; several minutes later it was presented
to him again and he quickly and easily gave the name. His
successful responses (at the age of 44 months) were, for the
most part, at the three-and-one-half and the four-year levels.
One certainly has the impression that this is a potentially able
child." When brought in during one of his phases of not
speaking, "he was very aloof and did not speak a word. He
was fascinated by the bridge of blocks built for his own little
car and smiled willingly, but would not try one himself;
he sat down once or twice, but each time became uneasy and
immediately pushed the chair away from him. He looked
out of the window a good deal and remained in a teasing
mood so that no satisfactory developmental picture could be
obtained. He resented all efforts to help him and pushed the
examiner's hand away. In general, he looked at everything
with a curious combination of attention and dreaminess. He
was not eager to leave, but went passively when told to go."

That Dick really had a most emotional interest in the integrity
of the objects to whose defects he referred casually became obvious
when, during his spells of silence or whispering, he could be observed creating a private world in which he could inquire about
missing things and be sure to get a comforting answer. Thus he
could be overheard asking himself, *"Has that car a spare tire?"* and
answering himself, *"Yes it has, Dick."* This (normal if transient)
method of dealing with observable fact he used also in matters of
conscience. "Dick, you must not do that.—But I want to do it.—
It is better not to do it.—But I am going to do it." Whereupon
the "adult" voice seemed to be giving in.

Dick seemed genuinely afraid that certain radiators were going
to bite him, and it will be one of the tasks of our play analysis to
find out why certain radiators seem to him to be animal-like, others
not. This manifest fear that something inanimate might have a
hidden mouth to bite him corresponded to the only recurrent dream
he liked to report, namely of a certain being to whom he gave a
strange name and of which he could only say that it had "no mouth."
Incidentally, he spoke about dreams as if they were real. Visiting
a friend, he would say, *"I was here last night and played with you."*
We know that many children indicate that at least in answer to
certain suggestive questions they are unable to differentiate verbally

between dream and reality. What interests us about this child is that he preferred to talk about such borderline experiences, often to the exclusion of all other topics. Cars often seemed to be animate beings for him. "It is too bad that motorcars have to sleep out in the street." For some time he has been differentiating also between men-cars and lady-cars, basing the distinction partly on types of cars which were driven by men or women of his acquaintance. This differentiation, however, overlapped with the one applied to all objects and based on their "yes" and "no" aspects, namely, whether they have a hole (a sink for him is a "no thing") or outstanding parts (a comb is a manifold "yes thing").

All-or-nothing people, who seem ready literally to pluck out the eye which offends them, are hard to deal with. When asked to *keep* it they may insist with equal radicalness on using it. Thus when Dick's parents noticed that to the detriment of his development he had decided to become in all physical and mental respects the likeness of his sister, they initiated a campaign for masculinity, insisting that to have a penis was practical and desirable and nothing to be ashamed of. He took them at their word. He exhibited his penis and, this prohibited, began to shout around his word for penis in a voice the masculinity of which left nothing to be desired; he began to lift the skirts of little girls and finally annoyed adult women visitors by looking at them from the frog's eye-view. The fact that the shouting of the word for penis occurred and was prohibited shortly before he met and annoyed the man who had no hair explains some of the intensity of his reaction to the grandmother's prohibition. For him, *to have a thing, to show it, and to use the word for it* meant three inseparable aspects of its possession. It was obviously intolerable to him that after he had tried in vain to be everything people seemed to like better than a little boy (namely, a pregnant mother, a little girl, etc.) he should meet even more powerful interferences when acting on the suggestion that he become a boy. Not only did he, as we have heard, begin to whisper, but he also wrapped his head in a sheet at night, tried to force his head into a toilet, etc. Biting became the dominant idea in his play; he threatened to bite not only his sister, but also himself, and actually was observed biting a dog's tail.

From such scant material, which gives the mother's complaints (somewhat ordered by us according to areas of expression rather than chronologically), we derive the following preliminary outline of Dick's personality: He is overcome by his drives at one moment, by prohibiting forces at the next; each time, however, an all-or-none attitude takes possession of him; similarly he changes his rôles of identification easily, although each time radically and completely. Thus in his subjective as well as his objective world he keeps rôles changeable, and parts detachable, introjects easily and projects easily. What danger he may be trying to ward off (if what we describe are defensive mechanisms, and not merely regression and disintegration) is only hinted at in the content of his phobia: *He is threatened by a being with a mouth, which in his dreams* (according to the undistorted wish-fulfilling character of children's dreams) *appears without a mouth.* Mouth and throat become the "zonal" emphasis in a world of dangerous have-nots (have holes) and detachable parts: he has spoken of biting ever since his last experiment in masculinity—at the height of the phallic phase—failed.

We cannot publish a detailed chronological life history of this child. Whatever historical data come to our mind as we observe the child's play will be reported in that context. We must concentrate on tracing the outline in playful and fearful acts of a doubting and often despairing infantile mind which has been unable so far to settle down to a clear differentiation of certain borderlines of individual and social existence. We shall see him concerned with *the differentiation between male and female, between ego and object, between animate and inanimate, between bodily coherence and fluctuating environment,* etc. As psychoanalytic experience and theory would lead us to expect such basic uncertainty will prove to be linked with an *oral complex,* i.e., the fixation on an easy regression to the wishes and fears of one of the incorporative stages. Beyond showing how this reveals itself in the child's play, we will avoid drawing diagnostic or prognostic conclusions from childhood material we are just learning to approach.

Whether the fault lies with the circumstances under which this material was won, or its inner affinity to the early stages of personality development, it is hard to present and doubtless even more difficult to read. The patient reader, it is hoped, will reach some point which can serve him as a bridge from his adult thinking to that of a disturbed infantile mind—and to that of stubborn observers who cannot bring themselves to dismiss "queer" material as meaningless.

The circumstances of observation and the nature of the material make the following methodological changes necessary:

1.   An account of the sequence of the child's acts will not be attempted. Instead, an inventory of behavior items (according to the classifications: toys, "life-sized" objects, people) will be given for each contact. Only occasionally will a reference be made which places an act nearer to the beginning or the end of a contact.

2.   Except where a coherent plot becomes discernible there will be no attempt to account regularly for the ideational content in the patient's fleeting play.

3.   In order to familiarize the reader with the character of this patient's play the inventory of the first three hours is given in toto before the single items are taken up for analysis.

1.   *Inventory of First Three Contacts*

a.   First contact.   Dick, who has never seen the physician before, seems from the very start to accept her in a matter-of-fact way. Pressing into her room, he only asks in a casual way, *"Are your eyes all right?"* and then eagerly, *"Where are the toys?"*—He immediately piles all the toys (except for a large truck with doors) into one box and carries them to the couch.—His mother, who comes after him to ask if it will be all right for her to go away, has to repeat her question before he gives a casual, rather impatient *"Yes."* She says goodbye, but he pays no further attention to her.

(1).   *Toys.*   Dick takes or points to a number of toys, and with one exception merely makes remarks about them instead of playing with them. He looks from all possible angles at the toy cars, his head close to them, and repeatedly makes the following remarks. "They have no spare tires." "Are they broken off?" "Did they ever have them?" "They are not meant to have spare tires, are they?" "It's all right, they don't need them." "Don't you touch them." "I don't like those cars." "I don't want to play with them."

He treats the red wrecker with a satisfied smile. "This car has two spare tires." "I like this one." He associates to it: "Mother's car has a spare tire."

"There is no water in the toilet." "We will leave the cover up." "We had better put it down again." "I don't have to go to the toilet." "Don't put any water in it."

Dick has left only one toy in the toy closet, a big red truck with doors. Near the end of the hour he says, *"I can't have it, can I?"* The physician says he can play with any of the toys. *"No,"* he says, and closes the closet door. Later he takes the truck out, opens its back doors, shuts them, and puts the truck back, saying, *"You mustn't touch it."*

He builds a garage for two cars; puts doors on it and two roofs; is pleased with it. After a little, he opens the doors with the intention of putting in two cars, then knocks the whole structure down, saying, *"I don't need it."*

(2) *Big objects.* Dick says, *"Does the chair come off?"* The physician thinks he means the swivel top and replies, *"No."* Dick says, *"Yes it does,"* and demonstrates by lifting the chair. "The table comes off too. You were kidding me when you said it didn't, weren't you?" (He lifts the table.)

He looks at the radiator in an intently exploratory way, eyeing the two ends with some anxiety, and says, *"There is no water coming out, is there? How does it work?"* The physician offers to turn on the steam. He seems alarmed and cries, *"Don't do it!"* The physician says, *"Tell me what you want to know about radiators."* Dick presses against the physician's knees and says in a confidential manner, *"I want to know about yellow radiators."*

Near the end of the hour Dick says to the physician, *"You mustn't take your dress off. I will spank you if you do."*

b. *Second (short) contact.* Dick again presses eagerly into the room the minute the door is opened and goes instantly to the toys. His acts and words are almost identical with those of the first contact with the difference that he handles the cars with more freedom and only once or twice comments on the lack of spare tires.

About the girl doll he says: *"She has no pants on. She has to go to the toilet. You make her sit on the toilet. She is all through."* He puts her in front of the basin to wash her hands, then puts her in the bath tub. (Her dress is sewed on.) "She is a naughty girl to be in the tub in her dress. She mustn't take her dress off."

c. *Third contact.*

(1) *Toys.* About the cars Dick says over and over: *"Do they have spare tires? Are they broken off?"* He points to little knobs and calls them spare tires.—He says, *"Have all wreckers two spare tires? I want to break them off."*

He sets the bathroom set up several times, each time hesitating to play with it. His eyes wander to the dolls, but he turns away again. Finally, near the end of the hour, he announces: *"The little girl needs a bath; she is sick."* He asks the physician to let the water run into the tub; he seems pleased and excited.

He opens the truck doors and says, *"I'd better shut them."* He opens them again and puts half a dozen toys in. He removes them again.

Dick again builds a garage with closed doors and runs a small car against the door as if it wanted to enter. The physician remarks, *"The car can't go through the closed door, can it?"* Dick opens the door, runs a car in and out and in again, leaves it for a while, then takes it out again and abandons the garage with the doors open.

(2). *Big objects.* About the carvings on the arms of the chair Dick says: *"They aren't feet, are they? They won't come off, will they?—They look like your hands."*

"I am afraid it will bite me." The physician asks, *"Who?"* Dick replies, with glee, *"The radiator downstairs."*

(3). *Physician.* Pressing against the physician's knees, he points to big gold buttons (resembling large raspberries) on her dress and says several times: *"I want to bite them."* The physician asks, *"Do you like to bite things?"* He replies, *"Yes, I like to bite sister. I am going to bite sister when I go home today."*—Shortly afterwards he says, *"I want to eat my dinner. Have you any crackers?"* Then he asks: *"People can't go down people's lanes, can they?"* The physician says, *"You mean the red lane?"* He replies, *"The yellow lane. Sister calls it a red lane. I call it a yellow lane.—Yellow is my favorite color."*

2. *First Contact: Analysis*
"A"
I
PHYSICIAN

Dick, who has never seen the Physician before, seems from the very start to accept her in a matter-of-fact way. Pressing into her room, he only asks in a casual way, *"Are your eyes all right?"* and then eagerly, *"Where are the toys?"*

II
TOYS

He immediately piles all the toys (except for a large truck with doors) into one box and carries them to the couch.

III

MOTHER

His mother, who comes after him to ask if it will be all right for her to go away, has to repeat her question before he gives a casual, rather impatient "*Yes.*" She says goodbye, but he pays no further attention to her.

"B"

I, II, III

No hesitance on seeing stranger (doctor) is manifested. His mother's departure is even urged with slight impatience. His interest in the physician is fleeting and temporary. All his eagerness is directed toward *having all the toys at once*.

In the macrosphere we thus see an exclusion of the mother, a passing by the doctor, an eager intrusion into the strange room; in the microsphere, an eager collection of all the toys (with the exclusion of one large truck) in one place.

The sentence, "*Are your eyes all right?*" is *D*'s individual way of saying, "*How do you do.*"

"C"

I, II, III

The impatience with which Dick leaves his *M* behind is in striking contrast to the usual mother adherence displayed by children brought for observation. One is immediately reminded of his reported tendency to pronouncedly deny his interest in persons, objects, or parts of himself to which he had clung the moment before.

His first likewise pronouncedly "casual" interest in *Ps* then, concerns a part of her body which to his mind (how seriously we don't know) could "come off." This remark recalls an episode: A barber not long ago happened to inflict a slight cut on Dick's ear, whereupon the boy would go to barbers only on the condition that they *did not wear eyeglasses*, as if to imply that persons who have detachable parts are more apt to mutilate others. It may be in keeping with such an idea that he feels safer with a doctor if her eyes are "all right." However, all this seems, for the moment, overshadowed by his eagerness to see the toys.

"A"

IV-VIII

Toys

Dick takes or points to a number of toys, and with one exception merely makes remarks about them instead of playing with them.

He looks from all possible angles at the toy CARS, his head close to them, and repeatedly makes the following remarks: *"They have no spare tires."* "Are they broken off?" "Did they ever have them?" "They are not meant to have spare tires, are they?" "It's all right, they don't need them." *"Don't you touch them."*

"I don't like those cars." *"I don't want to play with them."* He treats the red WRECKER with a satisfied smile. *"This car has two spare tires."* *"I like this one."*

He associates to it: "Mother's car has a spare tire."

"There is no water in the toilet." "We will leave the cover up." "We had better put it down again." "I don't have to go to the toilet."

"Don't put any water in it."

(Dick has left only one toy in the toy closet, a big red TRUCK with doors.) Near the end of the hour: *"I can't have it,* can I?" (The physician says he may play with any of the toys.) "No." Closes the closet door.

Later he takes the truck out, opens its back doors, shuts them, and puts the truck back. *"You mustn't touch it."*

He BUILDS A GARAGE for two cars; puts doors on it and two roofs; is pleased with it. After a little, he opens the doors with the intention of putting in two cars, then knocks the whole structure down, saying, *"I don't need it."*

"B"

IV-VIII

Dick reveals his interest and withdrawal in the following scale of approaches and avoidances.

Having *piled up* all the toys most eagerly, he does not play with them. He shifts his interest from one to the other, only to *discard* most toys with one or more remarks of a negative character.

He is positive about (*"likes"*) only the red wrecker (which has two spare tires where other cars have none) and *associates* to it his mother's car (the only reference to an object outside of the playroom).

He *manipulates* but does not play with the truck with two doors (which had been the only toy left behind in the closet).

He really *plays* only for a moment at building a two-door garage which, however, he *destroys* immediately.

At the same time he establishes a verbal adherence to the physician. In addition to referring to missing parts, he protests his disinclination to play with the toys and insists that such play is prohibited, either assumedly by the physician or expressly by himself.

"C"

IV-VIII

Dick's curve of interest and withdrawal recalls the strength of his initial attachment (eager incorporation) to persons and objects, and his seemingly unemotional dismissal and easy change of them.

As he wants to have all the toys but does not take the time to play with them, he insists on continuously talking with the physician without listening to her answers. His one-sided pursuit of a problem becomes most obvious where he dismisses as irrelevant permissions given by P_s and goes on establishing prohibitions. Thus, in spite of his confidential adherence and urgent inquisitiveness, Dick seems to be quite out of touch with the physician, while for the latter, it is not only hard to know what he means but also how seriously he is interested in what he means. Referring at random to the objects at hand, he is obviously speaking of some situation other than the one he presently shares with the physician.

A first hint as to what he may refer to is given in his questions in regard to parts coming off objects and to prohibited acts. These two classes of ideas in almost identical formulations are represented in the questions he asked his mother in rapid succession when she tried to assure him that his penis once and for all belonged to him: "Does sister have a penis?" *"Did she lose it?"* "Will she have one later?" *"Did she do anything naughty to it?"*

His assurances that the cars "aren't meant to have spare tires," that "they are all right," and "don't need them," correspond, then, to the answers the mother reports having given the boy: "Girls are meant to be the way they are," etc.

His whole attitude makes it probable that whatever he wants

to discuss here is related to a conversation he had with an adult. That "the cars are all right" as well as the prohibitions "not to touch them" are brought forward in the way of a now reassuring, now admonishing adult. As we saw, he not only discards *Ps*'s permission to play with (her) truck, but at the same time treats her as if she were not of age.

Thus, first eagerly interested in the toys, he gradually and individually denies his interest in any of them (except the wrecker with the double spare tires) and instead assumes the rôle of the adult who knows well that the play is forbidden, while the physician becomes a naughty girl with bad intentions. Are these intentions projected, i.e., do they represent his original play intentions? In any event, in creating this arrangement with an adult Dick goes one step further than he did in the monologues (overheard by *M*) in which he was two people all in one, the prohibiting adult and the stubborn child. He now assigns the infantile rôle totally to the physician while he becomes the prohibiting adult.

"D"

IV-VIII

The tentative nature of the first references to symbolic equations has been emphasized above. We are therefore stating them boldly here, going out from what seems to us the key to the patient's system of symbols.

Symbols. If small cars without spare tires are associated with *small human bodies with missing parts* (girls, sisters), a truck and a garage are larger bodies and potential *receptacles for smaller bodies* (women, mothers).

Arrangement. Dick, afraid to play because of the meaning the toys have for him, denies his interest in them; he takes unto himself the attitude of the selecting, prohibiting, and reassuring adult and assumes (projects?) naughty intentions in the physician.

"A"

IX, X, XI

Life-sized objects: Chair, Table, Radiator. "Does it *come off*? (CHAIR) (Physician thinks he means the swivel top and says, "*No*.") "Yes it does." He demonstrates by lifting the chair.

"The table comes off too. You were *kidding* me when you said it didn't, weren't you?" (He lifts the table.)

Looks at RADIATOR in an intently exploratory way, eyeing the two ends with some anxiety: "There is no *water coming out* is there? How does it work?" (Physician offers to turn on the steam.) He seems alarmed, "*Don't* do it!"

(Physician: "Tell me what you want to know about radiators?") Dick presses against physician's knees and says in a confidential manner, "I want to know about *yellow radiators.*"

"B"

IX, X, XI

On the whole, as we saw, avoiding microcosmic play, Dick gives a more courageous interest to some life-sized objects. He does not discard them as he did the smaller objects, but elatedly proves by lifting them that two of these objects (chair, table) "come off." However, when shifting his interest to the radiator, he withdraws: "Don't do it."

Thus his general attempt at showing himself the courageous master of the macrosphere (i.e., of life-sized objects and of the physician) he fails when confronted with the radiator *which has apertures and a watery, noisy inside.* When speaking of this, Dick develops a more intimate bodily adherence to the physician than he does during the rest of the contact.

Verbally, he *"kids"* her in the macrosphere as in the microsphere he had disciplined and reassured her.

"C"

IX, X, XI

In IV-VIII we understood Dick's first reference to the small toys to mean that parts are missing, have "come off." He now demonstrates to the physician that life-sized objects "come off" in toto. These objects have *four legs,* one similarity with animals. The radiator's similarity with animals rests on the fact that he has a (*warm, noisy, water-filled*) *inside and apertures for intake and release.* Dick dares to touch chair and table, but not the radiator.

This brings to mind the explanation Dick's mother had for his radiator phobia. It appeared, she reported, after a *nurse had kidded* Dick to the effect that *a certain radiator* (it was yellow and had four legs) would jump at him and *bite him.*

Probably she used this as a threat in connection with some mis-
demeanor on his part.

It seems possible, therefore, that Dick in his first contact is
introducing us to two aspects of one and the same problem,
(a) can small objects (children) lose parts "which they need,"
(b) have big objects (animals? adults?) the intention of suddenly jumping at you (and biting)? These questions appear
in a conversational context which betrays deep mistrust in
and the anxious wish to experiment with adults' prohibitions,
assurances, and jokes: His dealing with small objects seemed
to lead back to a *reassuring conversation with his mother,*
his dealing with big objects to refer to the *nurse's threat.*

"D"

IX, X, XI

1. *Symbols.* Chair, table, radiator; fourleggedness, occasional fourleggedness, apertures, warm touch, inner noise:
Bodies which move and bite.

2. Years ago a nurse had said a radiator would bite him.
"She is only kidding," his mother had reassured him. This
episode is represented with *displacement* (chair, table, which
do come off, instead of radiator), reversal from passive into
active (the physician is kidded and is shown that certain
objects *do* come off), and *denial* (of his fear). The arrangement fails in the case of a radiator, the original object of
his phobia. We see: Dick *believed in the nurse's threat more
than in his mother's reassurances.*

"A"

XII

PHYSICIAN

Near the end of the hour, to physician: *"You mustn't take
your dress off. I will spank you if you do."*

"B"

XII

After the short bodily adherence, Dick's interest in physician
again appears fleeting, surprising, teasing. She is small and
inclined to uncover herself; he is big, and assumes the punishing tone of an adult.

"C"

XII

During the first contact Dick's verbalized interest in the physician's body has proceeded from an organ extension (eyeglasses) which we assume to stand for the part they cover (eyes) to the clothes which may be taken off, revealing the *whole body*. This reflects two of the three foci of interest in inanimate objects, namely, the *partial* focus, "coming-off" parts of small objects; and the *total* one: the "coming off" of big objects.

A third focus, namely, the "insides" of larger objects which could enclose the smaller ones, has not appeared in relation to the physician's body. But we have noticed that all the extreme moments of the contact referred to receptacles. It was the big truck that was *completely ignored* at the beginning of the contact when Dick was so eager to get all the toys (—and to ignore mother and physician). His *only play* concerned the two-door garage which he destroyed, and *open anxiety* was obvious only when the working inside of the radiator was referred to. —(Has his fear of certain radiators originally been the fear of women's bodies? If yes, why?)

"D"

XII

Symbols. As there is a symbolic equation between toy cars and children, there is one between life-sized objects with four legs and animals or adults. The danger threatening the small beings is that something may "come off" them; the danger going out from big beings is that they may move and (at least so says his radiator phobia) bite.

Arrangement. The warning given the innocent physician not to take her dress off, again uses the projective-introjective arrangement which typified the whole hour. *He speaks as if she were intending to do the "naughty" thing he has in mind.* This is as far as the transference has developed during the first contact.

"E"

XII

If we review Dick's behavior with objects so far, we find three themes represented: (1) it is not permissible to touch

small cars (children) with missing parts (genitals); (2) it
is not permissible to touch big cars and other receptacles (women) which can harbor small cars (children); (3) it is dangerous to touch large inanimate objects (animals, women?) that
have apertures and an inside. In order to see the dangerous
ideas behind the avoided objects and acts we may connect
tentatively: 1 and 2: a girl is being born from within a mother;
1 and 3: missing parts on small bodies have been bitten off
by a dangerous big object; 2 and 3: inanimate and animate
receptacles are female; both have insides and dangerous
apertures.

3. Second (Very Short) Contact: Analysis

"A"

I

REPETITIONS

Dick again presses eagerly into the room the minute the
door is opened and goes instantly to the toys. His acts and
words are almost identical with those of the first contact with
the difference that he handles the cars with more freedom and
only once or twice comments on the lack of spare tires.

II

GIRL DOLL AND BATHROOM

"She has no pants on. She has to go to the toilet. You
make her sit on the toilet. She is all through."

Puts her in front of the basin to wash her hands; then puts
her in the bath tub. (Her dress is sewed on.) "She is a
naughty girl to be in the tub in her dress. She mustn't take
her dress off."

"B"

This is the longest interest Dick has attached to any one
toy so far. Ideational content: Dirty, *naughty*, exhibition-
istic girl is taken care of and reproved. Microcosmically the
girl is *put into a receptacle* (an act symbolically avoided the
day before). This is done in coöperation with the physician.

"C"

Like Mary in her second hour, Dick is somewhat changed.
The physician's impression is that he seems to accept in their

existing form the cars without spare tires, an impression that goes well with his maternal play with the girl doll. He is motherly today, perhaps an identification with the physician who the day before disproved his fearful expectations and proved not to be a doctor but a maternal friend.

On the other hand, the girl dolly seems to be pretty naughty —whether she does or does not take off her dress. She has inherited the naughtiness which during the first contact appeared partly in denials and was partly projected on the physician.

"D"

Arrangement. Dick and physician are united in the maternal care for a naughty child. According to our expectations (which Mary did not disappoint) this more concentrated microcosmic interlude should free some expansive energy for a clearer macrocosmic representation of Dick's wishes.

4. *Third Contact: Analysis*

"A"

I

TOYS

Over and over: "Do they (CARS) have spare tires? Are they broken off?" Points to *little knobs* and *calls them spare tires.*

"Have all WRECKERS two spare tires? I *want to break them off.*"

Sets BATHROOM SET up several times, each time hesitating to play with it. His eyes wander to the dolls, but he turns away again. Finally, near the end of the hour, he announces: "The little girl needs a bath, she is sick." Asks *Ps* to *let water run into the tub,* seems pleased and excited.

Opens TRUCK doors. "I'd better shut them." Opens them again and *puts* half a dozen *toys in.* Removes them again.

Dick again builds a GARAGE with closed doors and runs a small car against the door as if it wanted to enter. (Physician remarks, *"The car can't go through the closed door, can it?"*) Dick opens the door, runs a *car in and out and in again,* leaves it for a while, then takes it out again and abandons the garage with doors open.

"B"

I

Dick's interest, though still fleeting and finally always dis-
carded, remains with each item for one *positive* or *aggressive*
statement or move *beyond the first contact's* self-imposed limits.
The little have-not cars still have knobs that suggest the possibility there may have been or there some day may be more;
while the proud wrecker tempts him to break off his double
parts. —Toys are put into the truck, cars without spare tires
into a garage, and a (sick) girl into the bathtub. Verbally
there is an increase in positive statement.

"C"

I

Before he again disposes of the toys in his usual fleeting,
listless way, Dick adds something positive or aggressive to
his repetitions, as the following comparison shows:

First Contact	*Third Contact*
Cars "They have no spare tires."	"Little knobs are spare tires."
Wrecker "He has two spare tires."	"I want to break them off."
Truck "I must shut it."	Puts toys in.
Bathroom "Don't put any water in it."	"Let water run into the tub."
Garage Destroys structure before putting cars in.	Runs a car in. (Does not destroy the garage.)

The evaluation of the car knobs, in the generally more
hopeful atmosphere of this hour and if viewed in the context
of the other symbolical treatment of toy cars, corresponds to a
typical self-comforting infantile reaction to the observation of
sexual differences: Little boys and girls often expect a penis
to be growing inside the girl (the clitoris providing the girl
with a tangible hope) while little boys expect all nipples to
become breasts. Both vain hopes contain, as is so often the
case, some biological truth. The hopeful reference to these
knobs is, then, a belated symbolical expression of that one idea
in the conversation with his mother which had not been taken

care of in the first contact, namely, the question: "Will she (sister) have a penis later?"

It is interesting that this item, in the context of a general slight expansion of *Spielraum* in this hour occurs in connection with a temptation to devaluate the overcompensatory red car by making him lose what was his distinction. Dick's inclination to sacrifice his proudest possessions (tummy, penis) in order to avoid friction, and to atone for his aggressiveness against his sister must come to mind. (We remember he had tried to pull off his penis at the end of a supermasculine period when he had been told he was "hurting the girls' feelings.") This suggests a defense mechanism of equalization.

"A"

II

CHAIR, RADIATOR

About carvings on CHAIR'S arms: "They aren't feet, are they? They won't come off, will they? —They *look like your hands.*"

I am *afraid it will bite me.*" ("Who?") With glee: "The RADIATOR downstairs."

"B"

II

In the macrosphere (as in the microsphere) Dick's increasingly gleeful interest remains long enough with the subject to reveal further dangerous associations. (*a*) The association between a potentially detachable part of one of the life-sized objects (the chair's "hands") and a part of the physician's body is frankly pointed out; (*b*) the expectation of being bitten by a radiator is mentioned for the first time "with glee."

"C"

II

During the first hour it was already obvious that there was a correspondence between the spontaneous remarks made about the life-sized objects and those addressed to the physician, the idea of the big organism with dangerous intentions being the connecting association. It is in keeping with the aggressive expansion in the microsphere that in the macrosphere a connection is created between an inanimate, life-sized object and the physician's body. The first contact gave reason to suspect that the transference was developing along this line. (Remember Dick's first question: were the physician's eyes all right—which meant—or did they come off?)

The exalted feeling of "living dangerously" which accompanies today's adventurous expansion (in the microsphere it was represented by the idea of his wrecking the red wrecker) is climaxed in the queer pleasurable anticipation of the very event which is the center of his phobia, namely, to be bitten by the radiator. It is this glee in Dick which was always one of the most difficult traits to understand. There is little obvious "masochism" in it; rather a playful question in view of the dangers of bi-sexuality: how would it be if the sexes could be interchanged—what would one lose, what win?

"A"

III

PHYSICIAN

Pressing against the physician's knees, he points to big, *gold buttons* (resembling large raspberries) on her dress and says several times: *"I want to bite them."* ("Do you like to bite things?") "Yes, I like to bite sister. I am going to bite sister when I go home today."

Shortly afterwards: "I want to eat my dinner. Have you any crackers?"

Shortly afterwards: *"People can't go down people's lanes, can they?"* ("You mean the red lane?") "The *yellow lane.* Sister calls it a red lane. I call it a yellow lane.—Yellow is my favorite color."

"B"

III

This is the longest and most serious concentration on the physician's person reported so far. With verbal frankness two themes are clearly revealed: a biting wish toward her "buttons" and a consideration of the question of whether one person can be swallowed by another. Spatially, then, both the themes which were—first dramatized with inanimate objects have found their way to the human organism: parts of a whole being bitten by-a whole; a whole being swallowed by a whole. Verbally the statements are clear and frank; he gives a direct answer to question, while he associates one of the home problems, his playful wish to bite his sister.

"C"

III

The expansion in positive statements makes him reveal a wish toward the physician's dress: to bite her buttons. If we confront this statement (as we did the preceding ones) with the corresponding remark during the first hour, we find opposed: First hour "Don't take your dress off"—This hour: "I want to bite the buttons." The impression is that this expresses an oral interest in the physician's breast (see *E*) although the surprising clearness of the statement can be expected either to hide an as yet undiscernible factor or to lead to bad consequences, such as a belated disruption.

At home Dick has voiced for weeks a wish to "bite his sister's tummy." If we remember that he talked first of his "nice fat tummy" when his mother was pregnant (and that his tummy became devaluated after an unproductive hospitalization for a tonsillectomy) we realize that tummy once meant the bulging aspects of femininity and probably included the breasts as the outside of that big inside out of which the babies come, the very idea which we felt he symbolically approached and avoided from the start.

"D"

III

1. *Symbols:* Little knobs on cars—potential (detachable) organs (penis, nipples) on girl's body.

Buttons on physician's dress—nipples on woman's body (which one wishes to bite).

Yellow lane in yellow radiators	=	red lane in bodies	=	nutritional canal

Life-sized, four-legged objects—female organisms (by whom one expects to be bitten or swallowed).

Arrangement: After having microcosmically arranged during the second contact for the little girl to be the naughty child and for the physician and himself to be identified in standards and function in regard to such children, Dick dares to rearrange the whole inventory outlined during the first contact. (*a*) He establishes equality of equipment among the sexes: the knobs of the have-nots will become sizable parts, the spare tires of the have-too-muches can be broken off. (*b*) The cars are put into the truck, the sick girl into the bath; of

this the system of symbolic equation used so far admits only
one interpretation: the small sister is put back into the mother.
(*c*) People can not be swallowed by others; he is not afraid
of the radiator (the nurse was only fooling).

(Are these conditions under which he can express [in trans-
ference] his biting impulses toward his mother's body?)

"E"

III

1. On the afternoon of the day of this contact, Dick's
nursery school teacher makes an observation which indicates
that the interest in the female breast actually is uppermost in
the patient's mind on this day and is on the surface of his
consciousness, although already subject to the defense mechanism (introjection of prohibition) which we saw especially active
during the first contact: Dick asked the teacher whether the
buttons on her dress could be unbuttoned. Then he pulled her
dress apart without unbuttoning it; he "seemed eager and
tense." When the dress opened a little, he suddenly withdrew
and said, *"No, I can't look in."*
2. The dominating conception in all this play seems to be:
there are haves and have-nots in the biological world (yes-
things and no-things) and these two groups, in various forms
of intercourse, make use of their various extensions and inlets.
This mutual use seems to imply a danger to the inviolability
of the body as a whole: The mouth can suck and bite the
breast, the penis force itself into the body, the baby swell the
"tummy" and force its way out of it. These possibilities appear
doubly dangerous if one is ignorant or incredulous of the inner
or outer laws which are said to inhibit adult bodies from des-
troying one another and, on the other hand, possessed by impulses—in this case an overwhelming compulsion to think and
talk of biting and an equally overwhelming fear of being
bitten and robbed.
3. One could have made an interpretational statement to
the child at this point, indicating that behind his kidding terrifying ideas were hidden; that these secret ideas had given a
traumatic reality to the nurse's "kidding"; that it would be
worth while talking over what he meant by biting and what
the nurse had meant, etc.

5. *Fourth and Fifth Contact*

After the third contact, in which he had just revealed to the physician certain wishes and fears concerning the *biting* and *swallowing* of one human being by another, Dick contracted *croup*. If not genetically meaningful, this event must have secondarily assumed an unfortunate meaning, namely *oral* (throat) *punishment* for him. When, ten days later, he arrived for his fourth contact, we find him *whispering,* shrinking from self-expression, and armed against temptations as well as punishment. It takes only one more contact, however, to bring him back on the road toward further oral revelations. In order to let his extreme form of shrinking, self-limitation, and encasement stand out against another unfolding of his biting fantasies (which are now familiar to us) we shall briefly contrast, without detailed analysis, the most interesting corresponding items of the two contacts.

6. *Fourth Contact: Analysis*

"A"

Dick is not as eager as usual to enter the room. He has not taken his heavy snow suit off, seems extremely pale and apathetic and *speaks only in whispers.*

The physician suggests that he take off his snow suit and offers her help. He refuses, whispering, "I will keep them on anyhow. *I can sit out here until I take them off.*" From time to time he smiles at the physician, but stops as soon as she smiles back.

After a while he enters the room with all his clothes on. When asked whether he is hot, he whispers, "*I don't want to take them off;* just my sweater." Takes cap off so that sweater can be taken off; *puts cap on again* and keeps it on; he is plainly hot and uncomfortable for the duration of the contact. For the most part he wanders around, or moves back and forth on knees.

At one point he suddenly becomes more active; puts all square BLOCKS IN A ROW, end to end, and producing aphonic noises shoves the line of blocks along the floor by pushing the rear blocks.

Then he builds a GARAGE, runs the little red wrecker into it, and shoves the line of blocks so that they *block the garage* and, lying on his stomach and whispering, gazes into it.

Looks under GIRL DOLL'S skirts and examines her sleeves. Puts her in the bath tub, then on the floor. Puts BOY DOLL beside her. Puts *boy in| tub*. Puts *a block in front of the tub*. Lying on back, examines TRUCK intently. Suddenly in a *loud, clear voice*: *"That isn't a truck!"* He points to a little wheel that hangs down from the underside of the truck. (Physician asks, "What is it then?") *Whispering* again: *"It isn't anything."*

"B"

His interest is first concentrated on *himself* and on keeping himself enveloped in clothes and excluded from the physician's room. Then in sudden moves, while still keeping himself in a fortress of clothes, he is playing for moments with more concentration and more independence than ever before. He does not destroy or discard, but (whispering) watches his play arrangements. Autocosmically enveloped and without voice, he puts the *wrecker* in the garage and the *boy* into the tub and *blocks* both with blocks.

Verbal. Whispering and aphonic noises. The statement, "I can sit out here until I take them off" contains a *self verdict* in complete identification with an illusory adult judge. The only loud statement contains a *complete negation*: A truck with a spare wheel isn't a truck—it isn't anything.

"C"

The interrogation and bodily adherence to the physician is broken in this hour. Withdrawn into himself and enveloped in his clothes, he is able to concentrate on longer independent microcosmic play than before. The play is, in a certain sense, *narcissistic* in that he represents in the microsphere what happens in the autosphere: the objects of interest (himself, wrecker, boy-doll) are encased.

(Is he afraid the physician will examine his throat? The past has not given him any reason to expect this, nor has he himself ever treated the observer as a "doctor.")

"D"

Autosphere	*Macrosphere*	*Microsphere*
1. Head covered with cap. Body enveloped in clothes. Voice covered by whispering.	Detained in waiting room.	Beloved red wrecker and boy doll in receptacles with exit blocked.

The boy is unborn, (not the girl).

2. *Arrangement.* Dick today is completely identified with the voice of conscience. In the first hour he had projected all guilt content onto *Ps*, in the second hour onto the girl doll. In the third hour he had admitted aggressive wishes while already offering atonement. He now arrives at a deadlock of complete self-restriction and revengeful stubbornness: If I am not going to take my clothes off, I cannot enter the room and play. Therefore, I am not going to take them off. Dick's mother reports that she had blamed his carelessness in running around with too few clothes for his croup. The self-encasement of this contact, therefore, seems overdetermined, a queer mixture of self annihilation (punishment for last hour's references to the physician's body and implicitly his mother's body), security in self-restriction (he cannot do any harm) and stubborn, vengeful over-obedience (I am not supposed to have few clothes on,—I shall have too many on). That the overdetermination is necessary to produce the performance, is obvious from the fact that this extreme behavior does not occur at home (where his sickness spoke for him) but at the physician's office. It allows us to see some of the components of those "whispering" episodes because of which Dick was brought for treatment: the pious overdoing of a prohibition both as a defense against temptation and a veiled vengeful satisfaction. The whole mischievous energy pent up in such dramatized self-restriction becomes obvious in the following "criminal" features of the fifth contact.

7. *Fifth Contact*

"A"

Enters room, *lively, talkative,* with hand (through clothes) on genital. *"The floor doesn't come off, does it?"*

"You (PHYSICIAN) *haven't any penis."* ("That's right.") "Ladies haven't." *"Sister hasn't any penis."*

"I'll show you mine." *Exhibits himself.*

"You undress the GIRL (DOLL). You bite her tummy, her hand, her arm, her head, her feet, her behind."

(Pointing to FATHER DOLL): "I am going to take his hat off!"

"B"

The relationship between the microcosmic behavior of the

day before and this contact's macrocosmic behavior is clearly
one of complete reversal. Whether or not his self-encasement
was a relieving atonement for the weakness of the flesh or—as
an infantile Nirvana—a triumph of that weakness, today he
manically challenges the dangers which he fears most deeply.
His questioning and teasing in regard to things which "come
off" or part of which "come off" assumes a truly macrocosmic
form: at least the floor on which we stand won't come off!
Consequently the autocosmic fears only symbolically expressed
in the previous contacts are now clearly referred to and disproved: I can touch and show my penis! Such safety assured,
he not only does not shy away from the idea that girls have
been robbed and are bitten by women—he enjoys the idea.

It is interesting that it is in the context of such a disproval
of autocosmic dangers that he pays attention, for the first time,
to the father doll: he threatens to take off his hat (in dreams,
according to Freud, a penis-symbol). Of further interest is
the contemporaneousness of self-encasement and voicelessness
in the fourth contact, and that of emancipation of voice and
exhibitionism in the fifth. We remember that his first whispering spells occurred on the occasion of his being forbidden to
talk about a man's hairlessness; this happened shortly after
he had been denied the right at the height of his phallic
period to show his penis, to shout his word for penis, and to
look underneath the girls' skirts because "it hurt the girls'
feelings." The voice which exhibited, as it were, the penis
in word-magic and hurt the feelings of female beings had a
phallic connotation in more than one sense: The shouting, it
seems, had not only *exhibitionistically conveyed the content
penis*, but also as a *functional expression dramatized the intrusive mode* (*intensity* of voice and probably *phonetics* of
penis-synonym) with the sadistic connotation of hurting girls.

About the time of these contacts the writer met Dick under
the following conditions. He went to Dick's town in order
to observe him in his play group. While searching for the
teacher he suddenly heard strange shouts and terrified yells.
Looking into a nearby room, which proved to be the toilet,
he saw the boy (Dick) *exhibiting his penis and at the same
time shouting* into the ear of a girl of approximately his age.
The girl was in a panic, he in a strange state of compulsive
acting without much affective participation. (Being visual
rather than auditory, the observer remembers Dick's facial
expression but not the sounds of what he shouted.)

"*D*"

1. *Symbols.* Formerly symbolic ideas referring to the female lack of a penis and his own phallic pride appear undisguised. The modal synonymity between *shouting* and *exhibiting* and between *missing part and bitten off part* is expressed clearly.

2. *Arrangement.* Manic challenge, suppression of voice of conscience, denial of fears.

"*E*"

If the observation had been continued at this point, the challenging of the father figure would probably have proved to be the beginning of the revelation of a complex of ideas connecting his father with the radiator phobia. Other items which lead beyond the intended comparison between the fourth and the fifth contact have been omitted here.

Because in most case abstracts the reader is aware of the lack of detailed accounts transmitting the "feel" of the observational situation, we are concentrating here on a few detailed accounts at our disposal. The reader will now doubtless feel that his hard-won familiarity with Dick's mind should be rewarded with an abstract of his further treatment and development. This cannot be given here. Dick was recommended for thorough child-analytic treatment for which it was necessary to wait until his family's impending move to a larger city. As this is being written the treatment is in process.

A second unsatisfactory aspect of a detailed clinical account would not have been improved by a continuation of our report. On closer observation clinical material becomes more elusive. Every moment of attention, every step in the analytic direction is apt to bring to light a new element which proves to have been all-pervasive from the beginning. Descriptive and analytic restatements are necessary; reconstructions and interpretations, as they gain in volume, change in structure.

What is it then that we have set out to show: the emergence of an all-pervasive and only intra-individually logical (i.e., psychological) complex of ideas which alone gives the single reported behavior items symbolic or metaphoric meaning. Play acts of the kind Dick produced before our eyes are, of course, continually produced by other children in other situations, where they may mean something else or nothing beyond their face meaning. Small cars can "mean" small cars—within less fixed and less rigid configurations asserting themselves over shorter periods and through fewer areas of expression: The *prolonged and expanded sacrifice of the "real meaning"* of surrounding objects for the sake of their metaphoric meaning within a vicious circle of magic ideas is the mark of an emotional arrest.

Dick's dominating ideas express an *"oral complex."* He not only often speaks of biting; he betrays in addition to the world of physical facts as he knows them to be, an image of a world in which the biting wish is universal, its magic consequences unavoidable. When he is in panic, it is because of a radiator that will bite; when he dreams, it is of a being without a mouth. When proud, he shouts; when depressed or oppressed, he whispers. In demonstrating the emergence of this complex in play contacts, we hope to have demonstrated how, with little interference from the side of the physician, the dynamic interplay of two pairs of psychological powerfields forces the complex to the surface, namely, the interplay of *resistance and transference,* and that of the *level of fixation and the level of arrest.*

To begin with the latter pair: The level of fixation is that system of ideas, wishes, fears, defense mechanisms, ways of thinking, differentiating, experiencing which belong to a certain earlier period of childhood and the magnetic power of which is apt to exert again its way of organizing experience and action whenever a consolidation on a higher level of experience and action seems blocked. In Dick's case the fixation level is the second oral (biting) period. His level of arrest, on the other hand, is the intrusive stage, the developmental stage which proves unsurmountable to him. Dick is so hard to understand not only because his level of fixation is genetically an early, structurally a primitive one; the greatest difficulty arises from the fact that his inner world combines and synthesizes contents and principles of organization derived from both the level of fixation and the level of arrest. Thus we find phallic trends expressed in terms of the oral level (of fixation): i.e., his phallic-locomotor aggressiveness and the problems of sexual differentiation are represented as temptations to bite female persons and the fear of being bitten in turn. It is the *intrusive mode* which characterizes for him the functions of both the fixation zone (biting mouth, hurting voice) and the zone of arrest (the dangerous and endangered phallus). It could be argued that such irradiation of the intrusive problem had its center in the phallic stage and only regressively mobilized oral associations. Certain data which cannot be produced here, suggest that intrusion was a problem from the start. However, as we would expect, the conflict of intrusion found its climax and caused a general arrest and disintegration at the intrusive stage.

Caught between the phallic and the oral complexes as though between Scylla and Charybdis, Dick is unable to see how he can avoid the point where these two complexes touch; namely in the idea of hurting a woman, thus both losing protection and provoking punishment. The concept of the world which he reveals and which is not understandable with ordinary adult logic is an attempt to *synthesize the level of fixation and the level of arrest in order to derive a design for self-preservation.*

In the contacts with the physician, then, this "private world" of the child only slowly asserted itself against a *resistance* which tried to isolate it by avoidances and to keep it in a symbolic and metaphoric disguise; only gradually was it represented in connection with the *physician's person.* We have seen that the various aspects of this connection were *transferred,* in a certain disguise and with wishful changes, from former experiences with relations to other women (mother, nurse) and did not originate in the therapeutic situation, except in so far as woman doctor—nurse—and mother—situations have common attributes: they all favor associations such as: child's unsatisfied interest in woman's body, child's secret wishes in regard to woman's body, woman's investigation of child's body, threat to child's body, etc.[14]

---

[14]In Mary's case we saw how the image "man who plays with me" overcame the doctor association and favored the transfer of her conflict with the temporarily less playful father; while John, armed against all doctors, could not help delivering the secret to me which belonged to his father. But the material, especially in regard to the confession compulsion expressed in "A", is influenced by the initial "doctor"-expectations of the child. In the psychoanalysis of adults, too, there is a situational connection between the patient's very first associations and memories with the enforced infantile position into which he is asked to revert: the position of lying down, the sacrifice of upright and aggressive motility, the suggestion to lay himself open psychologically before a person who in his turn guards his integrity, the suggested lowering of the critical threshold and of cultural standards in expressing uncritically the flow of association. If not a verbal suggestion, all this certainly represents a situational emphasis which should be kept in mind when evaluating the first selection of childhood material emanating from the patient's associations and resistances.

The inventory of symbols revealed in Dick's developing play-manifestations rather clearly indicates the boy's concern with situations in which biological haves are threatened by the oral eagerness of the have-nots. Beyond this, only further analysis would reveal the syntax which in the patient's mind gives this inventory some kind of logical order. The reconstruction of what in the patient's mind is the cause of, the condition for, the temporal successor or predecessor of other factors, and how such psycho-logic compares with the historical sequence of events is a task accomplished only with painful slowness. Up to now we know approximately what the patient is talking about; but we do not know what he is saying, i.e., whether he is reporting the past or imagining the future, and whether he is representing what he is doing in such a picture or what is being done to him.

One example of a possible historical reconstruction would be this: The boy saw his sister nursed. He felt strange urges and aggressive impulses, only parts of which probably stood out consciously, as wish for the mother's breast, anger at the sister's favored position, aggression against his mother, etc. Factors of his stage of development (intrusive, locomotor, phallic), of his constitution (oral? schizoid?) and of his personality development (projective and introjective mechanisms) gave this wish dangerous connotations. For example, unlike his sister, he had teeth, a fact which may have been actually pointed out to him. This would be a danger threatening his mother.[16] However, his thoughts seemed also dangerous to his sister as it meant to take her nourishment away, an idea which fused with the other wish, namely, to send her back into the mother's body. His projective introjective ways of experiencing, then, intensified by the oral problem he was faced with, caused him to experience not only what mother and sister would feel if victimized by him, but also made him expect that they wanted to do to him what he wished to do to them.

It may have been during attempts to experiment with and to synthesize in play, theories, phantasies, and strange habits, such ideas of attacks and counter-attacks (in which he alternately identified himself with a dangerous mother and a small, toothless, penisless

---

[16]The first 20 hours of Dick's psychoanalytic treatment were signified by the fact that he had every toy bite every other toy, with two exceptions: *a baby doll and a toy cow never bit one another.*

baby) that the nurse helped by her threat to create a focus for all his anxieties in a radiator phobia. The idea that the radiator could jump and bite appealed to an always easily mobilized primitive level of the boy's mental life on which everything with noisy insides, a warm touch, pipe systems with water, etc., whether inanimate or animate, was somehow identical; while, like all objects of phobias, it also made more tangible, more impersonal, and more discussable, those vague and secret fears which could not be discussed with the protecting adults because they concerned just these adults: the radiator stands for what the child could expect the adult (mother) to do to him if she knew what he secretly wanted to do to her. On the other hand, while an unseen source of danger, this hypnotically attractive phobic object by no means created comfort, and the efforts at eradicating and denying the whole conflict could not relax. Dick dreams of a being which has no mouth at all and we recognized some of his phantasies as picturing a world in which there are no differences between the sexes and between big and little: everybody has and is everything and there need be no envy, no threat. Thus, beside a fear world in which vague dangers are pinned down to tangible objects and into a context with some kind of logical structure, we also see traces of a wish world, another synthetic product of the child's despairing ego.

Other observers and the reader may have arrived at other possibilities of reconstruction. But if we ask at this point who is right, there is only one answer: the patient. Only continued work with him could narrow down possibilities to probabilities and bring about that psychological insight, the formulation of which creates the feeling of high probability in the experienced reader, and if transmitted to the patient, clears his vision into the past and vitalizes his expectation of the future.

E. Destruction and Restitution in an "Epileptic" Boy of Four

With the following description we merely introduce the second phase of treatment, namely, the period following the decision to proceed with the psychoanalytic procedure proper, and the time of first interpretations. With the focus shifted, we shall abandon the detailed representation used so far.

Fred was entering the disquieting period of locomotor and sexual development usually associated with the age of four somewhat prematurely before his third birthday; we have tried to characterize this period briefly above. Mentally, his development ratio was 125; he was especially advanced in his verbal expression. Physically excellently developed and well nourished, he was easy to handle—especially if, as was often the case, he was given his own way. Certain sadistic characteristics mainly expressed in teasing and occasional tempers had been outspoken for years; but nothing would have induced either his parents or his pediatrician to suspect the clinical syndrome which now suddenly emerged, namely, "epilepsy."

For some time Fred had seemed to try in provocative games and social experiments to see how far he could go in playfully hurting others and in suffering their reactions. Although he enjoyed exploring by play and error the outer limits for the manifestation of an obviously pressing aggressiveness, he had a low tolerance for situations in which he actually hurt somebody or was actually hurt by somebody. As his silent paleness seemed to indicate, such events forced him to suppress in too short a time and to turn against himself the overwhelming aggression for which he was trying to find a social form.

The tension created by these manifestations which were neither in quantity nor in quality really abnormal, was heightened when one day his grandmother arrived in town for a long visit. She was even more anxious than his mother lest he hurt himself or get hurt; and special restraint was put on Fred's activity because she was afflicted with a heart disease. Fred tried his best, but soon increasing complaints from the neighborhood indicated that he had found a new field of activity. When he hit a boy with a shovel, he was ostracised in the neighborhood. It was shortly after this social trauma that he again went too far in his teasing attacks on his mother and, finally, on his grandmother.

One morning, in the presence only of the grandmother, he climbed on a windowsill and threatened to jump out of the window. Startled, the grandmother tried to reach him but fell on the floor, for the first time in his presence suffering one of her frequent heart attacks; she spent several months in bed, seemed to recover, but suddenly died. *"When I saw him standing there, something hurt in here,"* she had kept repeating over and over.

A few days after the old lady's death, Fred's mother saw him pile up his pillows before going to sleep, in a way in which his grandmother had done in order to feel more comfortable. In the morning, at the exact hour he had been awakened five days before by his mother's crying over the grandmother's death, he was heard making strange noises and found in a terrifying attack. His face was white, his eyes glassy; he frothed at the mouth and gagged. Finally, he shook all over and lost consciousness. To his mother he looked like her dying mother, but the hurriedly called physician diagnosed his symptoms as convulsions, ascribed them tentatively to bad tonsils, and administered an injection.

Soon two further attacks (usually beginning with the twitching of the face and subsequent clonic convulsions on the right side) followed at intervals of four weeks and six weeks respectively. The first attack lasted 20 minutes, the second 45. Immediately after the third, which lasted more than two hours, Fred was admitted to the hospital where he was diagnosed as an "idiopathic epileptic." However, neurological examinations were entirely negative except immediately after the attack. Fred, they emphasized, was an excellently-developed and well-nourished boy of above average intelligence and remarkable sociability. Dismissed after a few days of rest and observation, Fred was free of attacks for several months until, after two relatively less violent seizures, he again had to be hospitalized because of an attack at the time of the anniversary of the grandmother's death. The diagnosis appeared gradually modified as *"Idiopathic epilepsy with psychic stimulus as precipitating factor"* and the patient was recommended to the Department of Psychiatry and Mental Hygiene where he received treatment first from Dr. Felice Emery and then from this writer. During these treatments there were many minor (mostly staring) spells; major attacks occured only five days after his psychiatrist "had gone on a long trip," i.e., had moved to another town, and again, a year later, five days after the present writer had "gone to the Indians," i.e., on a field trip.

I shall first report on the psychological development of the case and then quote a neurologist's interpretation of the medical data in the light of our study.

Fred's parents had tried to explain the grandmother's disappearance by saying she had gone on a long trip. The boy, in spite of having seen the coffin and having witnessed the family's mourning, accepted and clung to the version that the grandmother had not died at all. But children betray their knowledge of such over-eagerly accepted adult lies with an uncanny sense of humor. Thus, one day when his mother asked him for an object which he had mislaid he said, "*I guess it has gone on a long trip.*" During the same period in his nursery school he was noticed building coffin-shaped houses whose openings he would barricade in a way corresponding to a death configuration, generally observable in play and in rituals of primitive people. It seemed clear that the boy "knew" and that this knowledge (or what he tried to do to it) was the "psychic stimulus" the physicians were looking for.

Before every major or minor attack, Fred's aggressiveness would increase. An object would fly out of his hands, sometimes creditably "without his being aware of it" and strike somebody's head. The usually affectionate and reverent boy at such times would indulge in violent attacks against parents and against God. "Did grandmother have a good heart when she was a child?" "The whole world is full of skunks." "I don't like you, mother." "I hate God." "I want to beat God." "I want to beat heaven." After the attack the boy would indicate that he had experienced his unconsciousness as death. He behaved as if he had been reborn, smiling, loving, obedient and reverent—an angelic child.

I shall first present excerpts from Dr. Felice Emery's notes in order to contrast the transferences which the boy established to this woman psychiatrist and then to me. The following development in play of two dominant ideas; namely, "burning and attacking psychiatrist" and "building a castle" reflect, it seems, the *destructive-restitutive* conflict in the boy's mind.

1. *Excerpts from the Patient's First Ten Contacts with Woman Psychiatrist*

I·

Fred, asking psychiatrist to smoke a cigarette, becomes extremely interested in the way it *slowly burns down.* He asks *Ps* to smoke two more cigarettes and watches intently. "Why don't *you smoke the burning end?*" he finally asks.

While watching *Ps*, he touches the telephone and she is forced to give him the instruction that the telephone is not an object at his disposal. Shortly afterward he suddenly reaches for the telephone and seeing that *Ps* is *startled* he says teasingly, "I wasn't going to touch it: *I fooled you!*"

II

"I'm going to *make you smoke* every time I come."

When *Ps* picks up a toy on the floor, he moves a screen so that it falls over her. In great excitement he crawls under the screen (which he calls a *blanket*), yelling, "I'm climbing up on top of you." Then he tries to stand on the screen but breaks through, dropping one and a half feet. He *crawls in and out* through the hole and calls it a window.

In the afternoon, at home, wandering around in a daze "as if hypnotized," he asks his mother what the difference between people and animals is and seems especially interested in *animals which jump at others*, such as tigers and dogs.

(He is coercive, aggressive, intrusive in thoughts and acts which imply: making *Ps* smoke the burning end of a cigarette, startling teasing, fooling her and climbing on top of her. A sexual meaning is discernible—underneath the screen he tries to climb "on top" of the psychiatrist calling the screen a "blanket." Is he afraid of the animal, the tiger, in *himself?*)

III

"When I put the *screen* over you, were you all *burning up?*" "Was your house ever burnt up?" "My house was never burnt up." "I want to go to the toilet."

(Note the associations—sexual act: burning; burning body; burning house; also the urinary urge at this moment.)

At home, just before falling asleep, he again refers to an animal aggression. "Cats are made the same as dogs and dogs are made the same as cats." "Can dogs climb trees?" "Why do they like to *chase cats?*"

IV

"I would like to set the whole *building on fire.*" "I'm going to set fire to your skirt."

"Let's *build* a castle."

(Note the association—setting fire to building: setting fire to psychiatrist's skirt. In view of this repeated analogy, we may expect an analogy of—building a castle: building a body.)

In the evening, asking again where there are tigers, he says to his mother, "The night is attached to the day. The day is attached to the night. The sun is attached to the sky."

(The constructive idea of building a castle has a counterpart in that of a coherent universe.)

V

"Could you smoke the cigarette from the wrong (*burning*) end?"

"I'm going to *undress you.* I'm going to *burn you.*"

"Let's build a castle."

VI

"I want to smoke" (takes one puff anxiously). "That's enough.—Do *firemen* ever get *on fire?*"

Hits a cigarette with a bar. "Is it *dead* now?" (burning: dying) "What part of a cigarette burns?—What parts of a house burn?" (burning cigarette = dying cigarette; burned house = dying house?; burned body = dying body?)

Stamps his feet and yells, "I am not going to leave till you build a castle."

VII

"You smoke a cigarette while you build a castle." (The destructive and the constructive ideas merge; see VIII and IX.)

"Would you turn into ashes if you would burn?"

He throws a ball of plasticine at *Ps*, yelling "I will *hurt you* and you will hurt me." After she has "hurt" him, he puts the chair in front of her, "You are *in jail.*"

"*Please walk with a creepy walk.*"

"There was a *lady who fell out of the* hotel *window* and she broke her hands, her legs, her body, her head. Wasn't that terrible?"

"We don't need a castle today."

(He wants *Ps* to walk in a creepy walk, which means to be an old woman, and he makes her hurt him and be put in prison. Is this the inversion in play of the fear which governs him, namely, that he will be put in jail [coffin, dark place, tomb] for having killed his grandmother by playfully threatening to jump out of the window?)

VIII

He hits the castle, with the words, "Does that hurt?" (Confirms the association—house: body.)

IX

"You smoke four cigarettes at once and build a castle that is round and has a door at each end."

He tries to light a match by stroking *Ps*'s cheek and by placing a match in her nostril. "Let's have a big flame."

Three times *Ps* builds a castle and three times he steps on a table and jumps on the blocks. From there he tries to jump on *Ps*.

(Repetitions with "orgiastic" dimensions: four cigarettes burn; three castles are destroyed; he tries to jump on *Ps* and actually to set fire to her.)

On Day III, the first association of burning and coitus had been followed by the wish to go to the toilet. Ever since, the psychiatrist had noticed a certain genital excitability in the boy as manifested in his repeated sudden urge to urinate, and in his clutching his penis. She now gives him a first interpretation by way of asking him whether to burn something, to destroy something, and to scare or jump on a woman gives him sensations in his penis. She thus approaches what must be most unconscious and least communicable to him and, furthermore, can be assumed to be one of the outstanding etiological factors in his sickness, namely, the strong phallic-locomotor emphasis at the time of the grandmother's death (and ever since).

To this question, Fred, surprised, reacts much like Dick "*I wish I were a little girl,*" he says. Then, transferring this idea of partial self-destruction and self-victimization to the house, the representative in play of a restituted body, he points to one of the longer blocks on the castle and asks, "Why is this sticking out?" He pushes it back. "Will that hurt the castle?" "Have you got a saw? I want to saw this off." He pushes a long block against it. "Does that hurt the castle?"

(He thus seems to experiment with the two aspects of the possession of a penis: who is hurt more, the male who loses it, or the female against whom it is used?)

Ps does not give him this explanation but merely remarks, "A castle made out of blocks falls apart rather easily. It is different from a person's body which can not fall apart in the same way." "Why doesn't it fall apart?" he asks. "Because the body has grown that way itself; every part is needed." He doubts, not without reason: "You need your eyes. Will your eye drop out?" "No—your eye won't drop out." "When it gets black and blue—what happens then?" "If your eye gets black and blue it heals."

In leaving *Ps* on this day, Fred says to his mother in an enthusiastic tone, "It's the biggest castle we have ever built."

(The castle was not bigger, but the interpretation had made the restitution more convincing.)

X

With this reassuring contact the themes of burning and building lose their central position in Fred's play with the therapist. Another content, more clearly betraying the fear of the dead grandmother, takes their place.

(We consider the fact that the content changes and approachs pathogenic material more courageously, a sign that the right interpretation took place at the right time.)

Fred now plays that an imaginary *lady* who is far away tries to call up 15 times a day. He wants *Ps* to go over to the house of that lady and break her telephone because the lady tries to call and to tell him that she is going to come and set him on fire or that she is going to send a policeman to arrest him. (We remember he had tried to set the psychiatrist on fire and, in Hour VII had jailed her, asking her to "walk with a creepy walk.") "We had better go off *on a long journey* so that when she comes *she won't find us here.* We had better take twelve gallons of gas."

While the imaginary overland connection to the lady takes the center of his play with the psychiatrist, at home his interest shifts to communication with *heaven.* "How does God tell you to be good? Heaven is higher than the clouds." As if incidentally, he also for the first time begins to ask about his *grandmother,* what she would look like now, would she look old, etc.

Soon *Ps* thinks the time has come to talk about the grandmother. Using his suggestion to write his name on a blackboard, she asks for his father's name, his mother's name, his grandmother's name, and when he pronounces the latter with special tenderness, she adds quietly, "Your *grandmother died,* didn't she?" Fred explodes, "No, she didn't die—she went away—*didn't she go away? Why did she die?* She was sick in my house. Did she die in my house? Is she in my house now? Well, where is she? Do you mean that I will never see her again? Let me see her."

Ps explains to him the impossibility of his wish, and in spite of his seeming to lose interest abruptly, insists on telling him that he must be thinking that he had done some harm to his grandmother. He answers decisively, "No—I didn't do anything to her," but then acts out his confession, as most children and some adults do: He climbs on the table (a conference table), stamps up and down the full length of it, and yells, "Who is making that noise? Can they hear it outside? What will they do if it disturbs them? If they did come in I wouldn't be quiet." Then menacingly coming up to the end of the table where *Ps* is sitting, he suddenly crouches down, climbs into her lap, and says quietly and anxiously, "Why did I stop here?" *Ps* repeats her explanation.

In the evening of this day at home, the boy begins to mourn as if he had never heard before that his grandmother was dead. He cried incessantly, asked why the grandmother had died, and why they hadn't taken her to the hospital to save her. "I would like to open grandmother's grave and see what she looks like. I will bring all of the doctors in the world here to make her heart go again." And then, with a scientific sublimation of the destructive impulse, he exlaimed: *"I would like to cut her body to pieces and see what it looks like inside."*

In the night he *soiled himself.* The next morning he didn't remember what day it was or what time of the day, and after having vomited, he slept far into the day. To his mother he said, "Supposing you would break your neck, you know what I would do? I would put it together again."

2.

Fred's treatment was not completed when his first psychoanalyst left the city. She had been able to bring back to his memory the details of his grandmother's death and to discuss with him the phallis-locomotor tension of his maturational stage, which had made him associate aggressive and phallic intentions as characterizing a bad boy. However, it was obvious that other sources of tension of the period in question had not been verbalized. Also, as the psychiatrist suggests, it may be that the playful aggression allowed to this child in analysis made the transference too realistic and permitted the accumulation in Fred of guilt feelings concerning the psychiatrist similar to those concerning the grandmother. In any event, after the psychiatrist had left town, Fred began to speak of her with the same words which he had always used to characterize his relationship to his grandmother ("Why has 'my friend' gone away?"), and had a severe *epileptic attack* (the first one since the

beginning of the treatment) *five days* after the departure, thus repeating the pattern "dying five days after a beloved person whom
one had attacked goes on a long journey."

After this attack, I took Fred over for treatment. The difference
in the transference became obvious soon. Fred had a period of what
one might call an infantile homosexual panic. After the first hour
with me, he insisted in retrospect that at the time of his latest
hospitalization *men nurses* had *taken his temperature* all night and
didn't let him sleep. This of course did not correspond to the facts
since he had been taken care of entirely by female nurses who had
taken his temperature only once during the night. But to this
phantasy there corresponded the first game he played with me during my first contact with him. Out of plasticine he formed "snakes"
or "worms" and tried to get behind me so that they could bite my
buttocks. (Remember how, in his play with the woman psychiatrist
in a similar twofold representation he had jailed the old lady, then
phantasied that an old lady was going to jail him). Correspondingly,
at home, his relationship to his father changed. He would without
provocation repeat, *"Don't touch me, Daddy,"* and especially when
awakening from his nap he would experience and express moments
of depersonalization—"I don't want you to come near me, Daddy.
Where am I? Where is our home? I don't see well. Is everything
all right? Everything looks bigger. Something is hanging from the
walls awfully big and crooked." He also began to look intently at
his father, remarking, *"Grandmother looked just like Daddy."* (We
see that the man therapist not only attracted another [homosexual]
transference but by his very existence brought about the manifestation of the corresponding [previously latent] conflicts at home).

In the meantime I questioned the mother again about the weeks
preceding the first attack because it seemed that Fred's guilt feeling
was not entirely covered by the explanation of the crime which he
felt he had committed against the grandmother. Only against severe
emotional resistance did the mother reveal an incident which had
occurred about one week before the grandmother's dramatic heart
attack. A toy had "inadvertently" flown from Fred's hand, hit his
mother in the face and loosened one of her front teeth. Irritable
as she may have been because of the special pressure which the
grandmother's visit exerted on the home, and also worried for the
precious front tooth, the mother had punished Fred corporally for

the first time in his life. As she described this, Fred's transference
to both the woman psychiatrist and to me appeared in a new light
—the crime complex established in connection with the grandmother's
death obviously had irradiated, in retrospect and prospect, to include
guilt feelings toward both father and mother and expectations of
danger for and from the side of both. (It will be remembered that
against his father he never had dared to express aggression as he
had so liberally done with women.)

I shall report here the way in which the transference of one of
these irradiations manifested itself in his first epileptic (minor)
spell in our offices.

During the first weeks of his treatment with me, we had in
accordance with his wish played dominoes. The possession of the
double black, so he had decided, determined who had the first move.
If he were not in possession of it and whenever he lost a game,
he became angry and pale. I tried (as far as he, a good player,
let me) to increase the number of his defeats gradually, in the hope
of being able to observe the coming and going of an attack under
emotional conditions approximately known to me. One day the
threshold seemed reached. Fred had lost again and at a time during
the hour when he could not hope to make up for it. Suddenly he
got up, took a rubber Popeye doll and *hit me* in the face with it;
then he stiffened, got pale, his eyes stared for a fraction of a second,
and he vomited. He had hardly recovered when he said in a most
pathetically urgent tone of voice, *"Let's go on playing."* He hurriedly built up his domino figures in front of him in a rectangle
and in such a way that the signs pointed inward: he, their possessor,
would have to lie inside of his configuration (like a *dead person* in
a coffin) in order to read them. Fully conscious, he now recognized
the queer configuration and gave me the look of a cornered animal.
I pointed out to him that every time he hit somebody he felt that
he must die. He confirmed this by asking breathlessly, *"Must I?"*
I explained to him the historical connection between these feelings
and the death of his grandmother, whose coffin he had seen. *"Yes,"*
he said, a little embarrassed because up to now in spite of the
mourning episode he had insisted that the grandmother had gone
on a trip. I furthermore pointed to the similarity between his attack
on my face during a game and the attack on his mother's face a
week before the grandmother's fatal attack. It appeared that he

could not remember the attack on his mother while he seemed never to have forgotten the episodes relating to his grandmother. That *the mother, too, might die* as a consequence of the (earlier) aggressive acts and phantasies was obviously the deepest danger threatening him. This, too, was pointed out.

Beginning with this episode a series of interpretations used *specific moments* to bring *his fear of death into relation with his strong impulses and his low anxiety threshold*.

The effect of such interpretational steps can best be illustrated by an episode which occurred a few days after the interpretation reported above. In the afternoon Fred's mother, fatigued, was lying on a couch. Fred stood in the doorway and looked at her. Suddenly he said slowly, "Only a very bad boy would like now to jump on you and step on you, only a very bad boy would want that, isn't that so, mummy?" The mother, to whom I had explained some of the boy's problems, laughed and replied, "Oh no, quite a good boy might *think* that, but, of course, he would know that he did not *really want to do it.*" This conversation established a relationship between mother and son which made it increasingly possible for him to tell her, especially when he felt as if an attack were approaching, of his aggressions, anxieties, and religious scruples, all of which she learned to handle as well as her own attitude toward death permitted. At the same time she could apply in such instances certain preventive measures recommended by pediatricians.

We see what the interpretation had done. It had used the highly *affective moment* (*namely the repetition in transference of a scene which the memory resisted*) to verbalize for him his impulses against the protecting mother—impulses derived from the same source as those which had "killed" the grandmother and thus might bring about the mother's death. These impulses could now be admitted to consciousness, faced with the superior intelligence of his increased age, understood as more magic than real and even admitted to the mother, who far from either wildly punishing or lightly approving, understood and offered help. Such experiences are an inducement to further transferences, confessions, and conversations, which of course included Fred's aggressions against his father which consequently were most consistently transferred to the therapist not without leading to a major attack five days after this therapist, too, had gone on a trip (from which he returned, however). Thus, while *historical reality* had emphasized the grandmother's death as the trigger stimulus mobilizing Fred's epileptic reaction, *analysis* proved Fred's sadistic wishes against his mother and death wishes against his father to be the *psychological reality* of his maturational stage which had made him susceptible for the traumatic event of the grandmother's death. This misunderstanding of the causal connection of what had happened to the grandmother and what he had done to her was transferred and interpreted first; what he was afraid might happen to the mother because of his deeds and wishes, next; while the most-dreaded and most deeply repressed aggression against the providers, father and God (the latter now united in heaven with the revengeful grandmother), could be approached only later. During this latter stage, his persistent attempts at building configurations of a safer body and a safer world, led to the construction (Figure 4). At the same time he day-dreamed of a compromise with God: why not eliminate death and birth, he asked him. Let children grow up and down, up and down, indefinitely. The block construction says the same in spatial projection: from a firm fundament roads lead away in two directions, but both come back and close the circle of safety—an earthly infinity.

In the course of these events Fred's attacks became fewer and

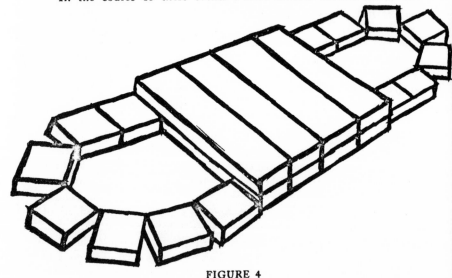

FIGURE 4

better predictable, drug applications could be reduced to a minimum and to well-circumscribed critical moments, and Fred recovered from minor spells more quickly and with less after-effect. We shall not predict that he will not have a minor attack now and again; but he may be spared major ones especially if the medical suspicion of a progressive lesion of the central nervous system proves unfounded. In any event, we have reason to consider it probable that psychosomatic vigilance can help such a patient to lead a normal life in which possible rare attacks are well isolated and for the most part predictable events.

Fred's case was chosen as our last example because it combined dramatic brevity with all the ordinary attributes of a situation in which an interpretation is warranted: The play has failed; the child is about to be overwhelmed by the guilt and the danger of the situation which he wants most to forget or to avoid. All defenses have proved inadequate, all attempts at restitution and atonement futile. The therapeutic situation has become the pathogenic situation, the therapist only one more evil. What seems needed is more cruel self-suppression, deeper regression, more radical repression. At this point the patient suddenly finds his experience put into words. The most human way (which always had seemed most completely impossible), namely, communication, now proves to be open.

However, once the first interpretation is given and its startling effects lived through, the child is conscious of the fact that the therapist understands or wants to understand more than he has been told, and that the patient is expected to coöperate in the verbalization of his suffering and what lies behind it. This brings with it complications and new resistances the description of which do not belong in this monograph.

3. Medical Note

During a short period of common affiliation with the institutions named below, I had the opportunity to discuss several case histories of epileptics with Dr. Frank Fremont-Smith, then Assistant Professor of Neuropathology in the Harvard Medical School and Associate Psychiatrist in the Massachusetts General Hospital. I have asked him to study my notes on "Fred" and to interpret the medical history in the light of the psychological study. I am indebted to him for the following abstract and statement:

1. The patient on first admission to the hospital was three years, one and one-half months of age. His family history showed nothing of significance to the present illness. Birth was full term, normal spontaneous delivery. The boy weighed 7.5 pounds, breathed and cried spontaneously. There was no cyanosis and no convulsions. The neonatal period was normal. No breast feeding. The developmental history too seems normal, with several attacks of sore throat and fever, once followed by a mild otitis media. At one and a half years of age and at two years of age the boy fell down a flight of stairs.

The first convulsion (five a.m.), two and a half months before admission, lasted 20 minutes; the second convulsion (one month later, 45 minutes. The third convulsion (at eighty-thirty p.m.) was described as follows: The patient cried out and vomited—twitching of eyes and mouth on right—then clonic convulsions of right arm and both legs—frothing at mouth—eyes turned to right—urinated—convulsion continued with violent twitching entire right side intermittently until morphine and scopolamine were given at eleven p.m. Twitching continued until admission at one a.m.

On admission and on subsequent days, physical examination was entirely negative with the exception that on admission, while in coma, deep reflexes and cremasteric reflexes were temporarily absent and there was a temporary *positive* Babinski reflex on the right. Laboratory studies, too, including lumbar puncture and fasting blood sugar, were negative with the exception of a moderate secondary anemia.

In the two and a half years following the first admission he had two convulsions, the first after finding the body of a dead mole, and the second immediately after inadvertently killing a butterfly. His sixth convulsion took place about a year later. He has continued to have "staring" spells and also occasional periods when he seems frightened and disorientated, usually preceded by vomiting. When he is entirely well he gets excellent grades at school and appears to make a good social adjustment outside the home.

The diagnosis from the medical record is idiopathic epilepsy with psychic stimulus as the precipitating factor and organic background not unlikely.

On several occasions the convulsions were observed to begin in the right hand, in twitching about the mouth, and once in the right eyelid. Some of the attacks have involved the right side much more than the left, especially the right arm, and the eyes have been observed deviated to the right. During one attack the right pupil was greater than the left, and after two attacks there was transient positive Babinski reaction, once on the right and once bilateral.

2. The term "idiopathic epilepsy" is used to describe a syndrome, fairly clearly defined clinically but, as the term "idiopathic" indicates, etiologically obscure. Examination of the brain at autopsy in such cases, may reveal congenital abnormality, the scar of birth injury or of post-natal injury or infection, or occasionally an unsuspected tumor, while not infrequently careful study fails to demonstrate any abnormality which could be considered as an etiological factor. The capacity to react with a convulsive seizure is normal for man and for mammals in general, as well as for many of the lower vertebrates, under appropriate stimulus such as electrical or pharmacological stimulation. The threshold for the convulsive response may be lowered by various irreversible structural lesions (scars, brain tumors, etc.) or by reversible chemical alterations (hypoglycemia, anoxemia, etc.).

An "epileptic" may be described as an individual whose threshold is permanently or temporarily lowered so that stimuli which in the average individual would not result in an attack (either grand mal or petit mal) frequently precipitate a seizure. The onset of an acute infection and the accentuation of an emotional conflict are common precipitating factors, which may become effective in cases with gross pathology of the brain, such as scar or tumor, as well as in the cases in which the predisposing factors are much more obscure.

In the case of the four year old child here described no final decision can yet be reached regarding etiology. The convulsions are typical grand mal seizures and the minor attacks consistent with petit mal and psychomotor seizures. The tendency for the attacks to start on the right side and to be most prominent on the right, together with the right Babinski reflex observed once, immediately after an attack, and the inequality of the pupils observed in another attack suggest the possibility of cerebral pathology (congenital abnormality, old scar or slowly growing tumor) in the left hemisphere as a predisposing factor, while the clinical history and the special psychological studies make it clear that emotional conflict is frequently the precipitating factor.

Whether such conflict as this boy exhibited could precipitate a convulsion in a child without disturbance of the central nervous system other than that accompanying the emotional conflict itself must remain an open question. It should be pointed out, however, that whether the conflict results in convulsion or other bodily manifestations, insight into the psychodynamics of the conflict is essential to the understanding and treatment of the emotional immaturity and social maladjustment which are on the basis of the conflict itself. The seizures from this point of view, when induced by emotional stress, may be looked upon as psychosomatic crises which in other individuals, differently constituted, might become manifest through other organ systems, cardiovascular, gastrointestinal, etc., including the psychic sphere, as in "psychomotor attacks" and "epileptic fugues."

IV. CONCLUSION

A.

The psychoanalytic attributes of our material are on the whole the mechanisms first described by Freud as resistance, transference, and regression. They appear in the interplay of social, verbal, spatial, and bodily forms of expression.

To begin with the verbal, the very first words spoken by our patients on meeting us, betrayed their dominant system of defense:

> *John*, we remember, appeared armed to the teeth. Asked whom he was going to kill, he answered, *"me"*—with one mono-syllable betraying the *"turning against himself"* of all the hate which his secret and other, less conscious reasons prevented him from expressing directly. *Mary*, however, did not say anything to the therapist until she had regained all her stubborn superiority. She only talked to her mother, in *lisping, whining* baby talk. We would not be surprised to find her use deliberate *regression* paired with stubbornness as a defense even in riper years. *Dick's* greeting *"are your eyes all right?"* makes the therapist the patient and the patient the therapist. It represents what Anna Freud calls "the identification with the (here potential) aggressor" and contains the *projective-introjective* mechanisms which prove so strong during later observations.—(*Fred's* first words are not recorded.)

Robbed or about to be robbed of the protective aura of maternal presence, how do our patients *act in space?*

> *John's* mother is nowhere near. While his eyes are evasive, his skin pale, he moves with unafraid strides. But he has surrounded himself with a *layer* of *weapons*. (He is the delinquent, afraid of further castration. His recent circumcision had been explained to him as a consequence of the fact that he had "played with himself," a fact which will have to be analyzed immediately after the resistance nearest to consciousness; namely, the secret, is worked through.) *Mary*, on entering with her mother, throws one mischievous glance across the room toward the therapist, then closes eyes and ears and almost *disappears* in the maternal skirt, holding the mother near the door. (She acts with hysterical dramatization and phobic avoidance. Ambivalent flight to her mother after a play disturbance with the father and with boys in a play group will prove to be her problem.) *Dick*, however, with hurried

663

determination leaves his mother and *passes by* the therapist as if not interested in her. (Interest in the female body will immediately begin to dominate his play.) *Fred,* finally after some diffused handling of the toys, *goes right for* the psychiatrist's body. (Playful attack, in his case, will prove to be the defense against his fear of being attacked and of suffering an "internalized" [epileptic] attack.)

It is in the metaphoric and symbolical use of toys that all these defenses are first caught off guard; in the *microsphere* the child does what he does not dare to do in reality:

John, in the macrosphere *armed against* doctors and police, in playing *"delivers" his secret,* although only in *metaphoric* allusion. *Mary,* the *bashful* one, has a moment of *mischievous hilarity* in pushing the toys and finally the toy train, although using a *protective extension* in doing so. *Dick,* so *indifferent* toward the mother and psychiatrist, has many *urgent questions* about the toy cars, in which he plainly *alludes* to the female body. *Fred,* the *killer,* passionately wants to build a house— to *restore a body,* as we were able to translate the *symbolism* of his play.

Each one of these *indirect admissions* in the microsphere is an element in a personal transference:

John, in delivering his secret metaphorically, gives the therapist what in reality is the *father's*. *Mary* betrays her playful interest in her *father* and in boys and (during the second contact) takes revenge on the therapist for a scene in which her father had reacted with irritability to her interest in him. *Dick* takes a little longer to express the more regressive wish to bite the *mother's* body, in the words, *"I want to bite your buttons."* *Fred,* after having "hurt" the therapist, wants her to "walk with a creepy walk" like the *grandmother*.

It is a question, partly only of words, which of the tricks of play language we are to call symbolic or metaphoric, which to consider analogies or allusions. A symbol, it seems, should be definitely of a higher order, very condensed and abstracted in its form, superindividual in its meaning and treated with a high degree of affectual inhibition and sublimation.

Mary, who suffered a play disruption when overturning the *toy train,* develops a raptured admiration for shining locomo-

tives. Her first question on seeing me weeks later concerns
the locomotive of the train which took me south. Her F in the
meantime had regained her friendship by joint visits to train-
yards. "Shining locomotive" has become a symbol of admired
paternal power.

It will take some careful study to denote how early true symbols
appear in play and what their fore-runners are. "Metaphoric" is an
appealing parallel to "transference" (metapherein—to transfer);
"allusion" has "play" in it (alludere—to play with). At the moment
I would say that the play acts reported are analogies to conflict
situations. The children unconsciously allude to them by transferring
their ambivalence toward their parents onto the therapist and by
representing other aspects of the conflict metaphorically in play.

But a child seems to be able to solve a problem in play or other
activities only inasfar as the traumatic event alluded to mainly consisted of an *enforced passivity*, a violation by a superior force.

> *Mary,* whose indignation with her irritable father and fear
> of operation are greater than her guilt, can "solve" her problem
> on the second day, at least enough to meet constructively an
> improved home situation.

Inasfar as the trauma involves "blood guilt," the primitive feeling
of having magically violated an ambivalently loved person, only a
conscious, verbally communicated "yes, yes—no, no" can bring relief.
This need, becoming urgent with the successful although first unconscious allusion to the conflict, drives some patients from the
treacherous play back into symptom and regression. At this point we
offer *interpretation* as a help toward communication.

> *John,* asked to name the uncles, answers with his symptom
> (defecation) and reasserts his defense—"*me.*" *Mary* becomes
> stiff, blind, and dumb with anxiety when the toy train over-
> turns. *Dick,* after having confessed that he wanted to bite
> the therapist's buttons, appears wrapped in clothes, in silence
> and in apathy. *Fred* gives me the first opportunity to observe
> one of his minor epileptic spells after having hit me in the
> face as he had done to his mother.

The play, we see, indicates the need which is both intensified
("ready to have its correlative feelings aroused") and in a state of

suppression; the *form of the disruption* alludes to the danger which would follow the fulfillment of the need.

> *John's* "me" indicates, that once his secret was revealed, something terrible would happen and that he preferred to be the victim. *Mary* dramatizes that, if she is too much of a tomboy and dares to envy the male his anatomical share, something similar to what already has happened to foot and genitals will, on the occasion of the threatened operation, happen to other parts of her body. *Dick* indicates that according to "an eye for an eye" he will be what his oral jealousy makes him wish his sister to be, namely, an unborn nothing. *Fred* in his arrangement of dominoes, confesses his expectation of death as a punishment or atonement for aggression.

All of this, of course, gives us only a first impression and allows only for tentative conclusions in regard to the *degree of emotional arrest,* the *depth of regression,* the *weakness of the defenses,* the *rigidity of conscience,* etc. On the one hand we weigh these impressions against the obstacles and weaknesses in the environment as transmitted by the parents; on the other hand, we have to reconstruct the degree of development attained when the arrest and the regression occurred, and weigh this positive aspect against the chances for our getting the environment ready to help the child beyond arrest and fixation when we succeed in making him set his face again toward the future.

B.

The goal of this description was a presentation of empirical data which (*a*) would allow the therapist and his study group to account for some of their diagnostic habits, and (*b*) could be of didactic-comparative use for non-therapeutic psychologists. However, clinical description, even where more skillfully handled, can only approximate such goals; and once such approximation is attempted, the focus shifts from the larger theoretical implications to the details of observation on which first conceptual steps can be based.

It seems advisable in conclusion to point to some of the practical and therapeutic aspects of our material.

Our "short stories" may have given the reader the impression that the psychoanalysis of a child is characterized throughout by high tension and by a rapid succession of dramatic insights. This is not the case. After our interpretations have led to relieving communication and to promising improvement, long periods follow which are quiet, peaceful, even dull. The child plays, builds, paints, writes, and discusses whatever he pleases as long as his guilt and anxiety allow him to do so. Such periods mean recovery for the child, more intimate and slowly growing insight to the therapist. But the therapist by no means accompanies the child's acts with running interpretative commentary. Interpretations to children are rare and on the whole underlie the following guiding principles. They point out symptoms of disruption throughout the patient's life and sum up the problem behind them as it has been reconstructed on the basis of recent observation. However, they do not translate to the child the meaning of any playfully or skillfully accomplished act. Verbal self-consciousness in conditioning connection with playful activities is not desired; for these very activities must help the child later to contact the fields of cultural value, in which alone he can really find a recovery without self-consciousness. There are also no attempts at arguing for an interpretation by transmitting to the child the details of its derivation. The interpretation will be accepted by the child if both the child and the therapist are intellectually and emotionally ready for it; which means for the therapist if he is in the right mood and frame of mind to put his insight into coherent, constructive, and understandable words.

This point deserves emphasis in conclusion. Throughout a tedious piece of writing I have paid compulsive attention to details of clinical reasoning. An analytical instrument was to be demonstrated. But to learn to know the properties and the range of an instrument is one thing—to learn to use it unself-consciously and firmly, another. It is good to be explicit for the sake of training; for the sake of therapy, it is necessary to act with intuitive regard for implied probabilities and possibilities. The scientific world wants to know *why* we are so sure to be on the right track; the patients only *that* we are sure. Few patients (and they are apt to argue and doubt) want to know whether or not our interpretations are scientifically true; most patients are satisfied that they feel true and that they *give meaning to suffering*. Except where the parent already has learned to expect this meaning from elaborate analysis and synthesis, increased scientific conscientiousness on the part of the therapist by no means necessarily conveys a feeling of security to him. Some groups of parents and adult patients, it is true, share the specialist's delight in new terminological, experimental, statistical rituals. The majority are bewildered by them. The conceptual frames of therapeutic habits, it must often seem to them, are like the microsphere in play, into which we project complex reality in order to have our wishes for omnipotence come true according to the less refractory microcosmic law and language. By reprojecting our interpretation into the macrosphere of social reality we are able to observe whether or not it provided constructive meaning within the patient's culture. By correlating it with those of other conceptual microspheres which have been longer and more consistently corrected by systematic experimental reprojection into physical reality we may see how scientific we are. But only if and where science will prove dominant over other sources of psychological strength will the scientific attitude in therapy also necessarily be the efficient one.

C.

It is an intriguing idea that even where nobody sees it or does anything about it children proceed to express their vital problems in the metaphoric language of play—more consistently and less self-consciously than they are able or willing to in words.

To be observed when playing is natural for children; it does not have to wait for the family's clinical surrender. If we can establish the language of play with its various cultural and age dialects[16] we may be able to approach the problem why it is that certain children live undamaged through what seem to be neurotic episodes and how early neurotic children may indicate that they have reached a deadlock.

This objective becomes important at a time when there is increasing awareness of both the extent of mental suffering and the impracticability and social deficiency of the alleviating techniques. Their results point to childhood as the possibly more economic time of correction.

---

[16]In connection with Jean Walker MacFarlane's guidance study (12) I am having the opportunity to collect in regular intervals microcosmic constructions of two hundred unselected children of the pre-adolescent age and to enter into a developmental and statistical appraisal of some of the play metaphors first encountered in clinical work. What sort of test can be based on such material is still a debatable question. At any rate ny contribution to H. A. Murray's *"Explorations in Personality"* is not as t has been titled a "Dramatic Production *Test"* but a clinical exploration.

The neurotic adult has usually made his choice of vocation and marriage companion on the basis of his neurosis. Both are endangered when that basis is reconsidered. The child's choices (except for that of his parents) are still preliminary; the changes we effect only replace changes which would occur with less planning. Furthermore, the adult patient usually develops a therapeutic dependency on his therapist, a dependency which every observing person will agree, often persists in the cured, and especially the much more frequent half-cured neurotic, in a form which differs from a neurosis only in the degree of terminological rationalization. One reason for this embarrassing fact undoubtedly is the impossibility, after one's analysis, of settling one's grievances with the childhood parents and of beginning life again, where the old road to isolation branched off. One has only one childhood. That which was merely repressed from consciousness, after having been reasonably developed and experienced, one may hope to liberate through analysis; but emotional impoverishment in childhood is incurable in later life, and to face the fact that one is crippled to the extent of having had the wrong childhood and to gain spiritually and intellectually from this fact is, after all, open to few.

The child's dependence, however, is his natural state. Transference in childhood has a different connotation; it is of shorter duration and less consistent, and what is transferred can usually be retransferred to the parents. The parents, in turn, are more accessible to correction and advice as long as they and the child are young, and small changes in the parents are often gratefully responded to by the child with obvious and far-reaching improvements. Thus, what is delegated to the therapist can be returned to the home before the child's personality development is completed and before all chances have been exhausted of identifying thoroughly with parents who are enlightened and live up to their capacity to love.

REFERENCES

1. *Psychoanal. Quar.*, 1935, **4**, No. 1. (Child analysis number.)
2. ERIKSON, E. HOMBURGER. Configurations in play; clinical notes. *Psychoanal. Quar.*, 1937, **6**, 138-214.
3. ———. Problems of infancy and early childhood. In: *Cyclopedia of Medicine, Surgery, and Specialties.* Philadelphia: Davis, 1940.
4. FRANK, L. K. Projective methods for the study of personality. *J. of Psychol.*, 1939, **8**, 389-413.
5. FREUD, ANNA. Introduction to the Technique of Child Analysis. Authorized translation by L. Pierce Clark. New York: Nerv. & Ment. Dis. Pub., 1928. Pp. 59.
6. ———. The Ego and the Mechanisms of Defense. London: Hogarth, 1937. Pp. 196.
7. FREUD, S. Analysis, terminable and interminable. *Internat. J. Psychoanal.*, 1937, **18**, 373-405.
8. ———. Beyond the Pleasure Principle. Authorized translation from the 2nd German ed., by C. J. M. Hubback. New York: Ballou, 1924. Pp. 90.
9. ———. Neue folge der vorlesungen zur einführung in die psychoanalyse. (His *Gesammelte Schriften*, 1934, **12**, 151-345.)
10. GITELSON, M., *et al.* Clinical experience with play therapy. *Amer. J. Orthopsychiat.*, 1938, **8**, 466-478.
11. KLEIN, (MRS.) MELANIE. The Psycho-Analysis of Children. New York: Norton, 1932. Pp. 393.
12. MACFARLANE, J. W. Studies in child guidance. *Monog. Soc. Res. Child Devel.*, 1938, **3**, No. 6.
13. MURRAY, H. A., *et al.* Explorations in Personality. New York: Oxford Univ. Press, 1938. Pp. 775.
14. SPENCER, H. Principles of Psychology. (3d ed.) New York: Appleton-Century, 1892. (2 vols.)
15. TOLMAN, E. C. Purposive Behavior in Animals and Men. New York: Appleton-Century, 1932. Pp. 463.
16. WÄLDER, R. The problem of the genesis of psychical conflict in earliest infancy; remarks on a paper by Joan Riviere. *Internat. J. Psychoanal.*, 1937, **18**, 406-473.

$\mathcal{C}$lassics In
$\mathcal{C}$hild $\mathcal{D}$evelopment

An Arno Press Collection

Baldwin, James Mark. **Thought and Things.** Four vols. in two. 1906-1915

Blatz, W[illiam] E[met], et al. **Collected Studies on the Dionne Quintuplets.** 1937

Bühler, Charlotte. **The First Year of Life.** 1930

Bühler, Karl. **The Mental Development of the Child.** 1930

Claparède, Ed[ouard]. **Experimental Pedagogy and the Psychology of the Child.** 1911

Factors Determining Intellectual Attainment. 1975

First Notes by Observant Parents. 1975

Freud, Anna. **Introduction to the Technic of Child Analysis.** 1928

Gesell, Arnold, et al. **Biographies of Child Development.** 1939

Goodenough, Florence L. **Measurement of Intelligence By Drawings.** 1926

Griffiths, Ruth. **A Study of Imagination in Early Childhood and Its Function in Mental Development.** 1918

Hall, G. Stanley and Some of His Pupils. **Aspects of Child Life and Education.** 1907

Hartshorne, Hugh and Mark May. **Studies in the Nature of Character. Vol. I: Studies in Deceit; Book One, General Methods and Results.** 1928

Hogan, Louise E. **A Study of a Child.** 1898

Hollingworth, Leta S. **Children Above 180 IQ, Stanford Binet:** Origins and Development. 1942

Kluver, Heinrich. **An Experimental Study of the Eidetic Type.** 1926

Lamson, Mary Swift. **Life and Education of Laura Dewey Bridgman, the Deaf, Dumb and Blind Girl.** 1881

Lewis, M[orris] M[ichael]. **Infant Speech:** A Study of the Beginnings of Language. 1936

McGraw, Myrtle B. **Growth: A Study of Johnny and Jimmy.** 1935

Monographs on Infancy. 1975

O'Shea, M. V., editor. **The Child: His Nature and His Needs.** 1925

Perez, Bernard. **The First Three Years of Childhood.** 1888

Romanes, George John. **Mental Evolution in Man:** Origin of Human Faculty. 1889

Shinn, Milicent Washburn. **The Biography of a Baby.** 1900

Stern, William. **Psychology of Early Childhood Up to the Sixth Year of Age.** 1924

Studies of Play. 1975

Terman, Lewis M. **Genius and Stupidity:** A Study of Some of the Intellectual Processes of Seven "Bright" and Seven "Stupid" Boys. 1906

Terman, Lewis M. **The Measurement of Intelligence.** 1916

Thorndike, Edward Lee. **Notes on Child Study.** 1901

Wilson, Louis N., compiler. **Bibliography of Child Study.** 1898-1912

[Witte, Karl Heinrich Gottfried]. **The Education of Karl Witte,** Or the Training of the Child. 1914